THE ART OF LOVE LYRICS
IN MEMORY OF
BERNARD COUROYER, OP
AND HANS JACOB POLOTSKY
FIRST EGYPTOLOGISTS
IN JERUSALEM

ISSN 0575-0741

CAHIERS DE LA REVUE BIBLIQUE

49

THE ART OF LOVE LYRICS
in memory of
Bernard Couroyer, OP
and Hans Jacob Polotsky
First Egyptologists in Jerusalem

Under the direction of:
Sara I. GROLL
Shalom PAUL
Marcel SIGRIST, OP

Edited by:
Krzysztof MODRAS, OP

PARIS
J. GABALDA ·et Cie Éditeurs
Rue Pierre et Marie Curie, 18

2000

ISBN : 2-85021-127-3
ISSN : 0575-0741

INTRODUCTION

Le 18 mai 1998, les efforts communs de deux Instituts de l'Université Hébraïque de Jérusalem - Institut des Études Juives, Département biblique, et Institut des Arts et des Lettres, Section d'Égyptologie, - et de l'École Biblique et Archéologique Française de Jérusalem aboutirent à une rencontre en mémoire du Père Bernard Couroyer, OP, et de Hans Jacob Polotsky, premiers égyptologues à Jérusalem. Elle succéda à deux autres rencontres, organisées dans les années précédentes[1], et eut lieu à l'Université Hébraïque. Elle fut intitulée « L'Art de la poésie amoureuse ». Nous aimerions remercier les organisateurs de ce colloque et spécialement le prof. Sarah Groll, de la Section d'Égyptologie, le prof. Shalom Paul, du Département biblique de l'Université Hébraïque, et le Père Marcel Sigrist, professeur d'assyriologie à l'École Biblique. Des remerciements spéciaux devraient être adressés aussi à l'Ambassade de France en Israël pour son aide financière dans l'organisation de ce rassemblement. Dans ce volume des *Cahiers de la Revue Biblique*, nous publions six conférences parmi les neuf qui furent prononcées au cours de la réunion.

Les communications présentées au colloque montrèrent qu'il est possible de parler de l'amour dans plusieurs domaines de l'existence humaine. Bien que son sens change légèrement dans la mesure où l'on passe d'un niveau à un autre, l'« amour » reste toujours un élément essentiel de la vie humaine sur la terre. Le premier type d'amour, celui qui touche naturellement le cœur humain, c'est l'affection qui existe entre l'homme et la femme. C'est le mérite de Yair Zakovitch, professeur à l'Université Hébraïque, de nous montrer l'intensité de l'amour qui unit le bien-aimé et la bien-aimée du *Cantique des Cantiques*. Le prof. Zakovitch remarque que le texte biblique peut avoir plusieurs interprétations, plus ou moins explicites. L'auteur biblique utilisa une langue énigmatique pour attirer l'attention du lecteur sur le contenu de son oeuvre et réveiller sa curiosité. Le livre biblique du

---

[1] Les conférences de la première rencontre ont été publiées par M. Sigrist, *Études égyptologiques et bibliques à la mémoire du Père B. Couroyer*, dans *Cahiers de la Revue Biblique*, 36, Paris 1997; celles de la deuxième, par I. Shirun-Grumach, *Jerusalem Studies in Egyptology*, dans *Ägypten und Altes Testament*, Band 40, Harrassowitz Verlag. Wiesbaden; in Kommission, 1998.

Cantique des Cantiques, comme d'autres poèmes sur l'amour qui font partie de la production littéraire du Moyen-Orient, utilise souvent ce genre de procédés rhétoriques. Le lecteur y découvre des rêves et de la fantaisie, et il lui est souvent difficile de distinguer la réalité de l'imagination. En langage figuré, le même mot peut posséder différentes significations ou, comme le dit Y. Zakovitch : "Lover and Beloved tease each other, as lovers do, and the reader, like the lovers themselves, must replay the words two or three times in order to penetrate the multilayered meaning". Le *Cantique des Cantiques* est une énigme susceptible de nombreuses réponses, et seulement plusieurs lectures du texte permettent au lecteur de découvrir le vrai sens du poème. La première lecture sera toujours superficielle et cachera encore la vraie beauté du poème.

Une histoire d'amour est souvent précédée d'un état de solitude. Le Dr Stefan Wimmer, de l'Université de Münich, découvrit ce phénomène dans le poème d'amour du papyrus égyptien Harris 500. Le couple devrait surmonter cette situation, mais avant d'arriver à l'union parfaite, il devra encore vaincre plusieurs obstacles. Cela s'explique aussi du point de vue psychologique : une personne qui est restée seule pendant longtemps, n'est pas capable de sortir immédiatement de son état de solitude, malgré ses désirs profonds. L'autre obstacle est parfois le manque d'enthousiasme de la part du partenaire masculin, ce qui peut être une conséquence de ses soucis matériels. La jeune fille essaie de le convaincre qu'ils tireront plus de profit en s'aimant qu'en s'enfermant dans leurs soucis. Ayant consenti à l'amour, tous les deux affronteront un autre problème : où pourront-ils se rencontrer ? Le garçon peut simuler une maladie et dire que la fille viendra lui rendre visite. Il peut aussi trouver l'occasion de la rencontrer pendant un rassemblement religieux. Cependant, le jardin est le lieu préféré, et d'abord, le sycomore, symbole de Hathor, déesse et source de l'amour. Rappelons aussi que dans le *Cantique des Cantiques*, la nature occupe une place privilégiée. À cette époque-là, une rencontre à la maison n'était certainement pas possible, soit en raison d'obstacles moraux et sociaux, soit pour des causes matérielles, comme fenêtres barrées et portes fermées. Le couple qui aspire à surmonter ces obstacles aimerait que son entourage accepte son amour mutuel. Finalement, le poème d'amour égyptien nous montre que l'amour, la solution des problèmes et la pleine réalisation de l'union entre les deux amoureux, tout vient de Dieu. Grâce à lui, ils arriveront à s'unir, tout seuls, lui en elle, et elle en lui.

Le prolongement de l'affection entre l'homme et la femme est l'amour pour leurs enfants. C'est le Dr Deborah Gera, de l'Université Hébraïque, qui attire notre attention sur ce domaine de la vie humaine. Dans des publications récentes, nous lisons parfois que des mères grecques n'aimaient pas leurs enfants. Peut-être la grande mortalité des enfants dans la Grèce antique affaiblissait-elle l'affection des mères qui pouvaient toujours se remarier et avoir d'autres enfants. De plus, l'abandon d'un enfant non désiré pouvait avoir la même conséquence. D'après cette pratique, c'était habituellement l'esclave, et non la femme elle-même, qui abandonnait le bébé soit dans un endroit écarté pour le laisser mourir soit sur une place publique où un passant pouvait le prendre et l'élever. Cependant, il faut remarquer que c'est le père et, à Sparte, les représentants officiels du peuple (et non pas la mère) qui décidaient légalement du sort du nouveau-né. Il faut aussi être conscient que l'abandon des enfants en Grèce est surtout « littéraire » et que la cruauté des mères de la mythologie, comme Thétis ou Médéa, ne devait pas nécessairement correspondre aux attitudes réelles des femmes grecques. Cette littérature, principalement produite par des hommes, reflète plutôt leurs perceptions et présente les tensions sociales qui existaient en Grèce entre la vie privée (*oikos*) et la vie publique (*polis*). Il y a aussi des textes montrant des mères grecques qui aimaient beaucoup leurs enfants. Ces exemples peuvent être considérés comme poésie amoureuse authentique et expression d'un véritable amour maternel.

L'amour au sein de la famille devrait être élargi à ceux qui vivent autour de nous. Le Dr Miriam Lichtheim, de l'Université de Los Angeles et de l'Université Hébraïque de Jérusalem, éclaire cet aspect de l'amour humain. La Bible nous commande : « Aime ton prochain » (Lev 19, 17-18.34). Comme le contexte l'indique, il faut comprendre les mots hébreux *ahikha*, ton frère et *'amitekha*, ton prochain, dans le sens plus large que le frère de sang ou le voisin le plus proche ; ce mot considère plutôt la communauté dans son ensemble. L'équivalent de ce commandement biblique se trouve, avec le même sens, dans le papyrus Chester Beatty No. IV, de la période ramesside (1300-1100 av. J.C.) La sagesse égyptienne enseigne : « Aime les gens pour que les gens t'aiment. » Certainement, le sens du mot biblique *ahav* et égyptien *mri*, dépasse ce qu'indique notre mot « amour ». Il peut signifier aussi « être utile » au prochain. De plus, les deux préceptes, soit biblique soit égyptien, commandent de faire du bien et d'éviter la vengeance. Ce refus de vengeance dans l'éthique égyptienne se fonde sur la conviction que Dieu récompense le bien et punit le mal. Par ce principe, les Égyptiens diffèrent des Grecs anciens qui vivaient selon la norme d'aimer les amis et de détester les ennemis jusqu'au cinquième siècle av. J-C. Le commandement biblique ne diffère de l'injonction égyptienne que dans son origine. Le précepte biblique est formulé comme un ordre divin et absolu, alors que les directives morales égyptiennes ne se réclament pas d'une origine ou d'une inspiration divines. Les dieux égyptiens ne parlent aux êtres humains que dans des occasions rares et spécifiques. Ils ne sont pas considérés comme enseignants des hommes, bien qu'ils soient les créateurs et les bienfaiteurs de tout ce qui existe. Néanmoins, ils veillent sur leur création et ils guident l'espèce humaine comme ses bergers.

Dans un sens encore plus large, l'amour peut assumer une nuance politique, et alors il indique l'union entre le roi et ses sujets. Le Prof. Sarah Groll de l'Université Hébraïque nous invite à réfléchir sur cet aspect de l'amour dans la période d'El-Amarna. À cette époque, la société égyptienne connaît de nouvelles tendances. Le Roi enseigne l'élite, et ses disciples doivent agir selon le principe de « Vérité et Justice » parce que leur Roi y est attaché. Ils l'aiment et veulent lui plaire, à lui personnellement, puisqu'ils savent que leur conduite rend le roi heureux, et qu'il déteste le mensonge. Pour sa part, le Roi est un enseignant qui est capable de susciter en eux ce désir de lui plaire, de le rendre heureux et même de l'imiter. Cependant, les sujets n'obéissent pas à un système de commandements apodictique et extérieur à eux-mêmes. Cette éducation est faite individuellement et n'est pas la conséquence d'un régime. C'est un instinct intérieur, qui se forme au cours du processus pédagogique, et qui les pousse vers la vérité. Le Dieu Aton aime le Roi, le Roi aime la vérité et les disciples aiment le Roi et la vérité. L'amour du Dieu Aton pour ses créatures ne vient pas d'un instinct sexuel. C'est un amour intellectuel, un fruit de la pensée philosophique et de la contemplation. Cet amour, dont la base est l'énergie solaire qui réchauffe tout, est une force qui unit les sujets dans une communauté homogène.

L'aspect social de l'amour trouva son expression pratique dans les milieux monastiques chrétiens d'Égypte. Le Dr Krzysztof Modras, de l'École Biblique, essaie de nous expliquer comment les moines coptes voulaient réaliser dans leur vie solitaire l'amour qui unit l'homme et la femme. Les deux premiers chapitres du *Livre de la Genèse* racontent que Dieu créa l'homme (homme et femme) à son image, selon sa ressemblance. Cela trouve sa pleine expression dans « homme et femme », car « il n'est pas bon que l'homme soit seul ». Ainsi, l'être humain fut créé à l'image de Dieu, mais cette image s'exprime dans une unité entre l'homme et la femme. D'une certaine manière, les deux se fondent dans un seul corps et ils demeurent dans le Jardin d'Éden où, étant tous deux nus, ils n'ont pas honte l'un devant l'autre. Les moines coptes, en abandonnant le monde et en menant solitaires une vie ascétique dans le désert, voulaient recréer ce premier état de l'homme et de la femme dans le Jardin d'Éden, état perdu après le péché. Cependant, les moines, à la place de l'idée du *Livre de la Genèse* qu'il n'est pas bon que l'homme soit seul, en proposèrent une autre, celle d'être *monos* qui devient une image de l'être humain parfait. Ils croyaient qu'il était possible de revenir au début de l'existence humaine et de trouver l'unité entre l'homme et la femme dans un seul corps. D'après eux, Dieu est capable de transformer l'être humain de sorte qu'il devient comme un ange, c'est-à-dire ni homme ni femme, quelque chose de commun, où l'image de Dieu a été recréée, à travers l'ascétisme et la gnose.

Krzysztof Modras, OP

SONG OF SONGS -- RIDDLE OF RIDDLES

In reading the Bible, one tends to seek out the ultimate sense, the simple meaning of the text. It is not my intention to plunge here into the vexed controversy of whether indeed there exists one single correct meaning to the exclusion of all others. Suffice it to say that the biblical text frequently invites its readers to uncover its ambiguity, with a single passage often lending itself to two simultaneous interpretations that are each made explicit to a greater or lesser degree.

The literary device of ambiguity is a common feature of poetry, as defined by D. Yellin: "Mishne ho-ra'a (double meaning) is used by the poet to surprise the reader, by employing one word to mean two different things, and the reader is drawn to discover what those two meanings might be."[1] I will cite but one of Yellin's copious examples: "Ah, those who chase liquor from early in the morning, And till late in the evening are inflamed by wine!" (Is. 5:11). The word *yadliqem* (= inflamed) describes the enthusing effects of the wine (see Hosea 7:5-2), but the stem *d-l-q* has the additional denotation of pursuit, thereby signifying that wine causes drinkers to pursue it night and day.[2]

Another example, also from Isaiah, is cited by M. Paran:[3] "Your men shall fall by the sword, your fighting manhood in battle" (Is. 3:25); the vocalization of the word מְתַיִךְ would indicate reading "your men", but the verse goes on to speak of those slain in battle, adding the second sense of מֵתַיִךְ, "your dead."[4]

S. Paul has recently published two articles with a wealth of examples for the use of paronomasia and other wordplay devices,[5] more than

---

[1] D. Yellin, le-torat ha-meliza ha-tanakhit, in: *The Collected Works of David Yellin*, vol. 6, Biblical Studies, ed. A. Z. Melamed, Jerusalem 1983, p. 254. For his discussion of this literary device, see pp. 254-268 and bibliography pp. 254-255.

[2] Ibid., pp. 258-259.

[3] M. Paran, "On Ambiguity in the Bible," *Beer-Sheva* 1 (1973), pp. 150-161 (Hebrew).

[4] For this example see ibid., pp. 154-155.

[5] S.M. Paul, "Polysensuous Polyvalency in Poetic Parallelism," *Sha'arei Talmon, Studies in the Bible, Qumran and the Ancient Near East Presented to Shemaryahu Talmon*, M. Fishbane, E. Tov (eds.), Winona Lake 1992, pp. 147-163; "Polysemous Pivotal Punctuation: On More Janus Double Entendres" in: *Texts, Temples and Traditions: A Tribute to Menahem Haran*, M. V. Fox, V. A. Hurowitz, A. Hurvitz, M. L.

enough to convince one that the biblical author was fond of enigmatic, equivocal language inviting the alert reader to unravel the double meanings enfolded therein.[6]

The Song of Songs wields ambiguity to attain unmatched elegance in this collection of some thirty refined erotic love poems, or *waṣfs*, unique in the Bible as to style, language and theme. The reader will discover these verses to be equivocal at times: some are dreams (e.g. 3:1-5; 5:2-6:3), others evoke a sense of phantasy (e.g. 1:2-4; 2:4-7),[7] leaving one uncertain as to what transpires in reality and what belongs to the realm of the imagination. At times the line between vehicle and tenor becomes blurred, with the same word bearing two different meanings -- the actual and the signified -- in the same poem.

This occasional obscurity is compounded by the quizzical tone bearing ambiguous messages: Lover and Beloved tease each other, as lovers do, and the reader, like the lovers themselves, must re-play the words two or three times in order to penetrate the multilayered meaning. The poems of the Song of Songs are riddles, and a riddle may have more than one answer. The reader who is content with one, superficial facet of meaning will miss the point and fail to reveal the humor that permeates the entire composition.

Let the willing reader, then, join us in a quest for solutions to riddles: you are invited to sit back and relax, but keep your linguistic sensibilities honed, and be prepared to smile along with the lovers. As we cannot read all the poems together, let us sample but several, to whet the appetite.

I. We begin with the shortest poem in this composition, consisting of only nine words in Hebrew:
Catch us the foxes,
The little foxes that ruin the vineyards --
For our vineyard is in blossom. (2:15)

Klein, B. J. Shwartz, N. Schupak (eds.), Winona Lake 1996, pp. 369-374. Both articles contain extensive bibliography.

6 On the devices of ambiguity and its influence on the unfolding of events, see my "Ambiguous Expressions in Biblical Narrative," in press.

7 See my *The Song of Songs - Introduction and Commentary*, *Mikra Leyisra'el*, Tel-Aviv Jerusalem 1982, pp. 27-29 (Hebrew).

But for its inclusion in Song of Songs, nothing would indicate its erotic nature: out of context, one might suppose this was a ditty chanted by children at play at a game of tag. The symmetry effected by repetition of the final word of the colon as initial word of the next colon, as well as by rhyme, impart a mischievous, light-hearted tone.[8] The context implies that the speaking voice is that of the young maidens: in the Song of Songs, the vineyard is a metaphor for a maiden (8:11-12) and for girlish innocence (1:6). An initial reading yields the impression that the women wish the foxes/men, who threaten their innocence, to be caught. While it is true that rapacious foxes ruin vineyards "in blossom" -- a delicate perfume wafts from the vine-blossom, especially in the early morning[9] -- (see also 2:13), the imperative is attenuated, even amused, for the threat is not grave - they are but "little" foxes, after all![10]

A second reading enables a different, contradictory understanding: no warning of lurking danger is raised here, but an invitation to the foxes to have their way with the women. The verb-stem *a-h-z* is used in the Song of Songs both for describing the beloved embracing her lover ("I held him fast, I would not let him go"; 3:4) and for the lover holding the palm-tree, metaphor for the beloved (7:9). *Lanu,* usually "for us," can also be the direct object "us" (see Lev. 19:18; 2 Sam. 3:30),[11] making this a command by the women to the men to catch them. This reading of the poem as encouragement to the men is supported by the use of *h-b-l,* "to ruin" but also "to conceive"; *h-b-l* appears in the latter sense in Song (8:5) and especially in Ps. 7:15:

הנה יחבל און והרה עמל וילד שקר:

"he hatches evil, conceives mischief, and gives birth to fraud." The mention of the fragrance wafting from the vine-blossoms is the climax of the

---

[8] On rhyming in biblical poetry, see W.G.E. Watson, *Classical Hebrew Poetry, JSOT Supplement Series 26,* Sheffield 1984, pp. 229-234.

[9] I. Loeb, *Die Flora der Juden,* 1, Wien 1924, pp. 72-73, 122.

[10] On the fox-cub as image of a lustful youth in ancient Egyptian poetry, see M. V. Fox, *Love Songs from Ancient Egypt,* Jerusalem 1985, pp. 18, 66 (Hebrew). "Little" may also be an allusion to the male genitalia; see "My little one is thicker than my father's loins" (1 Kings 12:10) and "That little organ a man has: starve it - it is satisfied; feed it - it starves." (Babylonian Talmud, Sukka 2b).

[11] See W. Gesenius, E. Kautzsch, A. E. Cowley, *Hebrew Grammar,* Oxford 1910, §117n.

maidens' seduction of the men, and in due course flower will become fruit, following the fox's visit to the vineyard -- the act of love.

The ambiguity of this riddle-poem may give recourse to a woman against whom accusations of being a seductress are leveled: she can always claim that she intended the other, innocent meaning - a plea for help and protection from the men!

II. The following example is also a female monologue: the maiden is telling the daughters of Jerusalem about herself, apparently apologizing for being different and inferior:

I am dark, but comely,
 O daughters of Jerusalem -
Like the tents of Kedar,
Like the pavilions of Solomon.
Don't stare at me because I am swarthy,
Because the sun has gazed upon me.
My mother's sons quarreled with me,
They made me guard the vineyard;
My own vineyard I did not guard. (1:5-6)

The negative perception of dark skin is due to its dryness: "My skin, blackened, is peeling off me; my bones are charred by the heat" (Job 30:30); "Now their faces are blacker than soot... Their skin has shriveled on their bones, It has become dry as wood" (Lam. 4:8). Still, she is not unattractive, says the maiden, but "comely." The stem q-d-r in "the tents of Kedar" conveys blackness: see especially Ben Sira 25:17 "Evil in a woman will darken a man's face and make it somber," but she is as beautiful as the pavilions of Solomon. By comparing herself first to the tents and then extending the metaphor to the synonym "pavilions," she puts herself on a par with the renowned wealth and sumptuousness of Solomon's possessions[12] (Is. 54:2; Jer. 4:20). Let them not be deceived by her dry, dark skin, says the maiden to the daughters of Jerusalem. She is well aware of her allure.

---

12 Solomon's wealth and sumptuous palaces are referred to in another poem: 3:7-10 and see also 8:11-12).

In the next verse, she implores them to pay no attention to her swarthiness, not to stare at her, that is: don't criticize (see Jer. 12:3), don't mock me (see Ps. 25:18; Job 41:26), don't be harsh in your judgment of me, for "the sun has gazed upon me" (Job 20:9; 28:7). The maiden is seemingly telling her companions: Don't look at me like that, for the sun has already gazed upon me. Several of the ancient translations interpreted *š-z-p* here to mean *š-r-p* (= to burn); perhaps linking it to *š-d-p* (= to scorch; Gen. 41:6).[13]

The maiden recounts how she acquired her desiccated look: her watchful brothers, ever intent upon preserving her honor, "quarreled" with her; by choosing *ḥ-r-ḥ* for "quarreled" (= *niḥaru*), the poet constructs clever wordplay between the fiery anger of the brothers and the sun's heat. For the link between *ḥ-r-ḥ* and blackness, see the above-mentioned verse from Job: "My skin, blackened, is peeling... my bones are charred from the heat" (Job 30:30).

The maiden's brothers instructed her to guard the vineyards, where her skin darkened, but the cause of their anger remains undivulged: the chiastic structure ("They made me guard the vineyards; / My own vineyards I did not guard") hints at cause and effect. Could she have failed to guard her own vineyard because she had to guard theirs? Perhaps she was forced to guard their vineyards as punishment for neglecting her own. "Vineyard" has two different meanings in its two uses here: in the first occurrence -- the vineyards the maiden was bidden to guard -- it is used in the literal sense, while the second is metaphorical - it is her innocence that she did not guard (2:15). The sister who brought shame and dishonor upon the family was banished by her brothers to guard the vineyards, where her skin blackened in the sun.

Are the maiden's words in fact a sincere apology for her inferiority to the milky-complexioned daughters of Jerusalem, sheltered in the shade of the city walls?

Further reading shows that the words of this riddle reveal a second, humorous interpretation, in which the country girl speaks with haughty arrogance: Black is not a sign of inferiority, black may indicate youth and vigor: "For youth and black hair are fleeting" (Ecc. 11:10).[14]

---

[13] See the Greek translations by Aquila, Theodotion.

[14] See C. L. Scow, *Ecclesiastes (AB)*, New York 1997, pp. 350-351.

By comparing her own beauty to the tents of Kedar, she affords the city dwellers a glimpse of the exotic world lying far beyond the walls, a world of nomad tribes who can be restrained by no boundary. She, the maiden, is as free as the wandering Kedarites, free to do as she pleases, with none but the sun to see. Her angry brothers banished her from home, but it is precisely her solitude that makes her liberty even sweeter, and allows her to be lax in guarding her own vineyard.[15]

The dusky, exotic rustic beauty arouses the envy of the daughters of Jerusalem, prisoners within the confines of the city walls and the strict conventions that prevail there.

III. Let us now examine two dialogue-poems; we will begin with the final poem of the book, consisting of the lover's appeal to his beloved, and her response:
O you who linger in the garden,
 Friends are listening;
Let me hear your voice.

"Hurry, my beloved,
 Swift as a gazelle or a young stag,
 To the hills of spices!"
(8:13-14)

An initial reading of this poem might lead the reader to believe that the lover's invitation has aroused the maiden's fury and spurred her to send him away. The book would then unexpectedly conclude on this jarring note, with the separation of the lovers.

The lover's address to his beloved: "You who dwell in the garden" indicates that he himself remains outside (see 4:12).[16] The lover wishes to take public pride in his beloved, not keep her hidden; he wants his companions to hear her voice. Such immature bragging is reminiscent of

---

[15] Another poem of the *Song* also expresses tension between the brothers bent on preserving their sister's honor and her own innocence: see 8:8-10.

[16] Similarly to "vineyard," which has two meanings in *Song* -- the literal one and the figurative one of the hidden female organ (see above on 1:6) -- "garden," too, can be the garden the woman sits in, as in our verse, but she herself can be the garden (4:12).

Ahasuerus, who commanded Queen Vashti to make an appearance before his guests so as to impress them with her beauty (Esther 1:10-11).
In Song, the lover is more tactful: he refers to his entourage as "friends,"
not "my friends" -- perhaps she is acquainted with them too, and says,
"let me hear your voice," not "let us." He seems to be ignoring his companions and requesting that she devote her song to him alone.

Like Vashti, the maiden too refuses her lover. She can compre-
hend his words in a different spirit than they were intended: listening to
a voice can mean obeying; he can be saying: my companions are listening you (= obeying), as I am, so let me hear your voice, i.e., command
me -- I shall do your bidding. For the use of listening to a voice in the
sense of a command, see for example, Gen. 3:17; 16:2.

And command him she does, humiliating him before his companions: "Hurry, my beloved", for my anger is fierce. However, let us not
take her admonishment too seriously, for if she is so incensed, why does
she still address him as "my beloved"?[17] Still, she is furious, and he
would do well to flee, as a gazelle (see, for instance, Prov. 6:5) or a
young stag. Another chink in her fearsome armor shows in the destina-
tion she stipulates for his flight: the hills of spices, suggestive and sen-
suous, most definitely do not sound like a penal colony.

The light-hearted threat draws the reader along to try his hand at a
completely different interpretation of the beloved's words: stag and gazelle are not only delicate, friendly animals; they are consistently used in
the book also as metaphors for the lovers. The maiden is not command-
ing her lover to flee from her, but to flee with her to a safe haven (see
2 Sam 27:4), away from his companions. Where might this haven be? In
another ambiguous verse, the beloved commands her lover: "When the
day blows gently, and the shadows flee, set out, my beloved, swift as a
gazelle, or a young stag, for the hills of spices (*bather*)!" (2:17) *Bather*
derives from *bithron*, the valley lying between two hills (2 Sam. 2:29).[18]
As yet, we still remain in the dark as to where "the hills of *bather*"
might be. At this point a third verse comes to our aid, from the conclud-

---

[17] Just as the warning against the foxes was playful rather than threatening, as they
are but "little foxes."

[18] See F. Brown, S. R. Driver, C. A. Briggs, *A Hebrew and English Lexicon of the
Old Testament,* Oxford 1966, p. 144.

ing words of a *wasf* describing the beloved's body (Song 4:1-7). The lover's gaze wanders down to her breasts: "Your breasts are like two fawns, twins of a gazelle, browsing among the lilies" (v.5). And the following verse opens with the same words as that cited above (Song 2:17), with the lover declaring: "When the day blows gently and the shadows flee, I will betake me to the mount of myrrh, to the hill of frankincense" (v. 6). The hills of spices, the hills of *bather*, the valley, are none other than her breasts; the beloved is enticing her lover away from his companions and his boasting, and inviting him to savor the pleasures of love with her.

Her invitation to her lover is a suitable conclusion for the book, with the union of the lovers taking place far from prying eyes.[19]

IV. In the next dialogue-poem, it is once more the beloved who has the last word, but the structure differs from the previous *wasf*. Here, the beloved speaks first, her lover responds, and she then concludes dialogue:
I am a rose of Sharon,
A lily of the valleys.

Like a lily among thorns,
So is my darling among the maidens.

Like an apple tree among trees of the forest, so is my beloved among the youths.
I delight to sit in his shade,
And his fruit is sweet to my mouth. (2:1-3)

The maiden begins by comparing herself to wildflowers found the Sharon region and the valleys, not particularly rare species, presumably; in any case, the precise horticultural identification is not of prime impor-

---

[19] The joyful conclusion of the book with the union of the lovers invites the reader to start reading it anew from the beginning: while the final poem has the beloved sending her lover to "the hills of spices," the scent of spices is invoked in the opening poem: "Your ointments yield a sweet fragrance, your name is like finest oil." (1:3). At the end of the book she bids him flee, and at the beginning: "Draw me after you, let us run!" (1:4). He mentions his companions and their interest in her, at the end: "Friends are listening to your voice" (8:13) while in the opening poem she speaks of the maidens' interest in him: "Therefore do maidens love you" (1:3).

tance to the understanding of the text.[20] Her words perplex the lover:
what is her purpose in calling herself a rose and a lily? Does she expect
the lover to object, and praise her beauty? This is indeed how he understands her words; he expatiates upon the mention of the rose, praising
her beauty: if she is a rose, other women are thorns, lacking beauty but
capable of nasty damage.

But no: this is not what the maiden yearns to hear. Her lover has
failed to solve her riddle. A woman comparing herself to a flower, especially a rose, expects to be plucked: "My beloved has gone down to his
garden, to the beds of spices, to browse in the gardens and to pick lilies.
I am my beloved's and my beloved is mine; he browses among the lilies." (6:2-3) Has the lover failed to unravel her secret because he is not
as bold as she is, too timid to take the initiative towards their union?
How can she carry out her purpose without shaming him? She starts out
her reply by returning his compliment in the same coin: "Like an apple
tree among trees of the forest, so is my beloved among the youths." The
apple tree is frequently mentioned in the Song of Songs (2:5; 7:9).[21] The
"trees of the forest" are those, which bear no fruit (Eze. 15:2; Ecc. 2:5-
6). Her compliment is therefore more generous than his, for although the
trees of the forest are not without value - they provide shade and wood -
the lover surpasses them. Not only does the apple tree possess the superior qualities of the trees of the forest, such as shade: "I delight to sit in
his shade"; it also bears fruit: "and his fruit is sweet to my mouth." By
elaborating upon his original compliment, the maiden alludes, in her
mention of eating his sweet fruit, to the act of love; cf. the maiden's
words to her lover elsewhere in Song: "His mouth is delicious and all of
him is delightful" (5:16). The maiden is so intent on joining her lover
that she speaks in the past tense (2:4), as though they had already been
intimate together.[22]

---

[20] For possible classification of the flowers in *Song*, see J. Feliks, *Plant World of
the Bible*, Ramat Gan 1966, pp. 234, 242-3 (Hebrew).

[21] On the classification of the apple tree see ibid., pp. 60-63.

[22] For this form of the past (perfectum confidentiae), see Gesenius (above, n.11)
§106n.

V. Our last example is a dialogue-poem in which the brothers tease their
little sister in ambiguous phrases, and she answers adroitly, solving their
riddles correctly by choosing the appropriate meaning.
We have a little sister,
Whose breasts are not yet formed.
What shall we do for our sister
When she is spoken for?
If she be a wall,
We will build upon it a silver battlement;
If she be a door,
We will panel it in cedar.
I am a wall,
My breasts are like towers.
So I became in his eyes
As one who finds favor. (8:8-10)

The poem has three couplets: in the first couplet the brothers paint an
apparently objective picture (v. 8a), and inquire how they will cope with
the future situation (v. 8b). In the second couplet they introduce two alternative scenarios and their own reactions (v. 9). It is unclear upon first
reading if both possibilities are one and the same, or opposites. The third
couplet is the sister's response to her brothers, in which she picks up
their metaphors and expands them: her "I am a wall" is the replique to
the beginning of the second couplet, after which she reacts to their observation that "her breasts have not yet formed" with the retort "My
breasts are like towers". There seems to be some discrepancy between
her perception of herself and that of her brothers.

    In the first couplet the brothers are discussing their sister among
themselves, ignoring her but speaking deliberately, knowing she is listening. They seem to be expressing concern for their little sister. Is she
very young, or merely younger than her brothers, or perhaps "little" is
not a reference to her age at all but to lack of sexual development:
"whose breasts are not yet formed." They are worried about the absence

of the badges of femininity so highly prized in erotic poetry (see, for instance 4:5; 7:9).[23]

If indeed this is their meaning, then "what shall we do with her when she is spoken for" in marriage (1 Sam. 25:39) may be an expression of genuine concern and embarrassment: should a man wish to speak for her, her shame will be made public. However, again, they may be referring to her age, without intending any criticism of her physical development.

Let us now address the hypothetical situations the brothers raise in the second couplet, and attend to their ambiguity. "If she is a wall" may refer to their sister's flat chest; but should she accuse them of insulting her honor, they can always claim that they spoke of her chastity, the hope that she would stand as stalwart as a fortress that no man can scale. The reaction of the brothers to the "If she be a wall" scenario also lends itself to the two interpretations: "we will build upon it a silver battlement" (see Eze. 46:23) may refer to a jeweled ornament shaped like a fortified city, similar to the City of Gold that Rabbi Aqiba had made for his wife (Babylonian Talmud, Shabbat 59 a).[24] The jewel would hide the humiliating absence of breasts, if we pursue the first interpretation of "wall," but we may also contend that the costly trinket would be fitting reward for a maiden's modesty.

If we now turn to the second scenario: "If she be a door" - we see that it can also, like the wall image, be a reference to the sister's flat chest. The brothers' solution is similar: "We will panel it in cedar," that is, they will fashion a form or tie[25] a panel of cedar, finest of woods,[26] to hide what is missing underneath. But if it is her chastity they are speaking of, we have yet another ambiguity. Door may be a synecdoche for wall: a gate within a wall: "a tranquil people living secure, all of them

---

[23] See: "When is a girl a minor? From when she is eleven years old and a day until she is twelve years old and a day" (Babylonian Talmud Yebamoth 100b). See also: E. Ben Yehuda, *A Complete Dictionary of Ancient and Modern Hebrew*, vol. 12, Tel Aviv 1951, p. 5881 (Hebrew).

[24] On jewelry of this type see S. M. Paul, "Jerusalem - A City of Gold," *IEJ* 17 (1967), pp. 259-263.

[25] For the stem z-w-r in the sense of fashioning a form, see B.D.B. (above, n. 18), p. 849.

[26] For z-w-r in the sense of "to tie," see B.D.B. p. 848.

living in unwalled towns and lacking bars and gates" (Eze. 38:11). The gates are fortification: "I will shatter doors of bronze, and cut down iron bars" (Is. 45:2); their solicitude in covering her with costly panels of cedar would express admiration and approbation. On the other hand, the door image might be the reverse of the wall, with the opening door a symbol of wantonness, which must be checked by the obdurate cedar, to keep the door locked to strangers.

The little sister hears her brothers out patiently, solves their riddles, then replies in a fashion that shows how cleverly she chooses among the various possible interpretations: I am a wall, replies the sister, choosing the wall, since it is an unambiguous emblem of chastity, over the door. "Wall" is a metaphor for chastity, in her understanding, and not a reference to her chest, for indeed she does have breasts. The brothers apparently know nothing of their sister. They haven't taken the trouble to take a good look at her for quite some time; had they looked they would have seen fine, firm breasts like towers. She picks up the thread of bellicose imagery, and to the revelation of her well-developed breasts adds another surprising disclosure: she has a lover, of whose very existence the brothers have hitherto been ignorant. "So I became, in his eyes, as one who finds *shalom* (lit. peace or repose)". Repose is used in this sense by Ruth to her widowed daughters-in-law, in adjuring them to marry again: "May... each of you find repose in the house of a husband" (Ruth 1:9) and "Daughter, I must seek a home for you, where you may find repose" (Ruth 3:1). Our poem substitutes peace for repose, since the sister wishes to teach her brothers that all the bellicose imagery (wall, siege, towers) is no longer necessary; she has found peace and security with her lover and the door opens, beckoning him in, as the laws of war in Deuteronomy have it, in speaking of a besieged city: "If it responds peaceably and lets you in ...." (Deut. 20:11).

Thus, over the many voices speaking in the love poems of the Song of Songs reigns peaceful repose, and all have a smile on their lips, with the easing of tension that comes with the realization that there are only mock crises in this composition. The supposed tension dissipates with the exposure of the multilayered meaning. The reader smiles too, with the thrill of discovery, the realization that he was deceived in his initial, superficial reading of the poem. Smiles, and a general optimism, are a fitting accompaniment for love: eroticism can be a daunting subject, and the playful ambiguity and mischievous wordplay in the Song of Songs set the lovers at ease as they do ourselves, lovers of erotic poetry and its riddles.

Yair Zakovitch
Translated from the Hebrew by Sara Friedman.

ANCIENT EGYPTIAN LOVE SONGS:
PAPYRUS HARRIS 500
New Insights into an Old Problem

for Samaher from Shechem

Introduction

The Papyrus Harris 500 (= British Museum 10060) is preserved over a length of 122 cm, height 19 cm, with the beginning and the end missing. The recto contains six complete plus two incomplete pages of love songs. These appear to be generally unconnected compositions loosely grouped in two collections of eight stanzas each (group A: nos. 1-8; group B: nos. 9-16). What follows is "the Song from the Tomb of King Antef", a poem of a different genre called "Harper's songs"; these draw a pessimistic assessment on the perspectives of the afterlife and conclude with a *carpe diem!*-message. In their advise to enjoy the pleasures of this world, this genre is not unrelated to the topic of love songs. The latter are then resumed with one complete song of three stanzas (group C: nos. 17-19), plus two independent, fragmentary stanzas (nos. 19A, 19B). The state of preservation is generally good, at some passages the papyrus tissue has thinned out into numerous netlike little lacunae, while at some spots a few larger pieces are missing. The writing is the hieratic uncial of the 19th dynasty.

The editio princeps was presented a century ago in W. Max Müller, *Die Liebespoesie der Alten Ägypter*, Leipzig 1899. Major studies followed with Siegfried Schott, *Altägyptische Liebeslieder*, Zürich 1950, and Alfred Hermann, *Altägyptische Liebesdichtung*, Wiesbaden 1959. Two recent studies: Michael V. Fox, *The Song of Songs and the Ancient Egyptian Love Songs*, Wisconsin 1985, and Bernard Mathieu, *La poésie amoureuse de l'Égypte ancienne*, Cairo 1996, will infra be quoted as "Fox" and "Mathieu" respectively.

While I was myself a student at the Hebrew University Department of Egyptology, Prof. Sarah Groll commissioned me in 1990 to check the published facsimile and transcriptions with the original in the

British Museum.[1] This, and an extensive study of the results with her in Jerusalem, resulted in some alternative new readings, a selection of which is presented here for the first time. This presentation is therefore widely indebted to Sarah Groll, even where it is not mentioned explicitly. What I owe to her is more, anyway, than I can tell. And the same holds true, I would like to add, for what Egyptology in Jerusalem owes to Sarah Groll.

What's before a love story

Not always, but still in many cases, a love story starts from a preceding state of loneliness. It seems that our papyrus contains a hitherto unrecognized reference:

B 10 (page 4, line 7), Fox: "The voice of the <u>goose</u> cries out, as he's <u>trapped</u> by the <u>bait</u>." Mathieu: "C'est la voix de la <u>sarcelle</u> qui s'égosille, <u>saisie</u> par son <u>appât</u>." (underlinings by me). The passage is commonly understood as describing a boy - "the goose" - caught in a love trap. While I will revert to the metaphor of the goose later, the word wʿjj.t, translated as <u>bait</u> here, deserves immediate attention. It has the determinative of a worm, which makes the surface meaning of a bait eaten by a goose plausible.

Sarah Groll has pointed out at *The Tenth World Congress of Jewish Studies*, in Jerusalem in 1990, that in another text, ostracon Nash 12, the worm serves as a phonetic writing for the same word wʿjj, which is to be taken for what it literally stands: <u>solitude</u>.[2] Our passage therefore has a double meaning: people listening to the song, regarding the written determinative, certainly understood the underlying meaning, namely that the person was <u>trapped/stuck</u> or perhaps also <u>fed up</u> with his <u>loneliness</u>. The word mḥw, translated as <u>trapped</u> by Fox, literally means <u>filled</u>. The

---

[1] I am indebted to Dr. Stephen Quirke for his kindness.

[2] S. Israelit-Groll, Ostracon Nash 12 and Chapter 5 of Song of Songs, *Proceedings of the Tenth World Congress of Jewish Studies*, Division A: The Bible and its World, Jerusalem 1990, 131-135.

boy or man may have experienced his state of loneliness like the fattening of a goose.

In the preceding stanza it is the girl who puns with the same expression $w^c jj(.t)$, written again with the worm determinative. She imagines birds arriving from the myrrh-country Punt:

B 9 (4,4), Fox: "The first to come takes my <u>bait</u>."

Mathieu: "Un oiseau ... vient en premier pour prendre mon <u>appât</u>."

What she actually expects is one who would take her <u>loneliness</u> away! She continues:

B 9 (4,5) "Watch out! We shall expulse it (viz. <u>loneliness</u>) at once. I am with you, I <u>alone</u>!" (own translation). She resumes the pun again with the word <u>alone</u> $w^c.kwj$, which has the same root as $w^c jj.t$, <u>loneliness</u>. However, before the two can reach this point of being together, alone with each other, there are yet all kinds of obstacles to overcome.

Problems in the way

The first passage quoted above, "The voice of the goose shouts, being stuck with its loneliness" (own transl.), continues somewhat unexpectedly:

B 10 (4,7-8) "Your loving me repulses me. <u>I cannot release it</u> (viz. my loneliness)" (own transl.) The second part, $bw\ rh=j\ sfh.t=s$, could alternatively be translated as "<u>I can't cope with it</u> (viz. with your love)." This way or the other, we are facing, as it seems, a psychological phenomenon, familiar to those who experienced it: a person who had been extensively lonely is not immediately capable of giving up his or her solitude, even though it is this what he/she aspires more than anything.

Other obstacles, not so much of a psychological nature (or are they?), are listed in the first preserved song, where the girl complains to her partner about his lacking enthusiasm:

A 1(1,3ff.) "Are you straying/uninterested, because you think of <u>eating</u>? Are you (such) a man-of-his-stomach? Are you straying because of <u>clothes</u>? I possess linen! Are you straying because of– " (own transl.)

The next word is badly preserved, and various suggestions have been made how to read it:

Fox suggests "... because you are <u>hungry</u>", which is not very convincing since we had this point already. Mathieu's idea "... pour de la <u>bière</u>" fits better. The positioning, though, is a little disturbing; one would expect food and drink coupled together but we have clothes in between.

My suggestion for this word is "... because of the <u>Nile</u>". *jtrw*, the Nile, stands for inundation and for what it gives to Egypt and her inhabitants: the economic means of living. After a short lacuna, the girl continues:

A 1 (1,5) "You may take my <u>breast</u> flowing over for you all its goods." (own transl.)

The metaphor of the abundant Nile becomes obvious here. The word:

read *mnd.t,* <u>breast</u>, might just as well be transcribed *mn.tjj,* <u>(pair of) thighs</u>: "You may take my <u>thighs</u> flowing over for you all their goods." (own transl.) The allusion would then refer to a promising offspring she is predicting him. Contrary to our modern Western assessment, numerous children have always been, in most societies, regarded as a blessing, insuring economic prosperity, rather than the opposite. What the man worries about is nutrition ("eating"), clothing ("linen"), and income ("the Nile").

The parallel with one of the best known passages from the Sermon on the Mount just confirms that these were the most basic needs one would think of in any given context: "Do not worry about your life, what you will eat or drink; or about your body, what you will wear. ... Who of you by worrying can add a single hour to his life?" (Mt 6:25). Curiously even the concluding advice of our girl to her partner is in a way reminiscent to the Gospel's observation: A 1 (1,5-6) "We profit more of a day of embracing [each other], than of a myriad's part of (your) <u>worries</u>!" (own transl.) The clue for this passage lies in the transcription of the until now not understood last word, as a strange spelling (pseudo group writing) of *ḥnḥ*, <u>fear, worries</u> [3]:

$$\bar{=} \text{𓇋}\text{𓄿}\text{𓇋}\text{𓎟}\text{𓏏}\text{𓏤}\text{𓈖}\text{𓏥}\text{...}\text{𓎡}\text{𓈖}\text{𓂋}\text{𓏏}\text{𓆑}\text{𓈖}\text{𓏌}$$

t(w)=n 3ḫ (m) hrw n ḥp.t ... (r) r3 ḥfnw ḥnḥ

The main problem: Where?

Once the two are agreed for love, they face another old problem: where to meet. In today's Western culture the answer can practically be "anywhere", and the problem is virtually reduced to the choice of "your place or my place?". In all other societies, however, at any time in history and still today in many parts of the world, social norms do pose serious restrictions, to varying degrees, to the possibilities of "dating". In the Egyptian love lyrics this topic is not a very prominent one - probably not because it would not have existed, but rather because it was so basic and obvious that it was not necessary to elaborate.

This obviously provides the background for a boy's plan to feign illness, confident that the beloved girl will then be among the visitors coming to look after him:

A 6 (2,9ff.) "I will lie down inside, and I will pretend to be ill; then my neighbours will enter to look; then (my) sister will come with them. She will startle the doctors. She understands my illness." (own transl.)[4]

Festival occasions

When a boy is sailing to Memphis and invokes Ptah, "Give me (my) sister tonight!" (A 5; 2,7), then this may express traveling to a distant lover; it may also hint at a popular opportunity to meet and mix with the other sex at a religious festival. The latter is definitely the case in stanza A 8, with a girl telling us that she has come to Heliopolis for public celebrations around the Ity-canal. "My heart is set at those who are going to prepare the booths". It seems that she is expecting "him" to be among "those". "Then I will see the entry of (my) brother. He is heading

---

[3] Cf. Erman/Grapow, *Wörterbuch der ägyptischen Sprache*, Berlin/Leipzig 1926-1963, III, 115,7.

[4] For this topic cf. also J.G. Griffiths, Love as a Disease, in: S. Israelit-Groll (ed.), *Studies in Egyptology Presented to Miriam Lichtheim*, Jerusalem 1990, 349-364.

for the 'Houses of the Gate (?)' " (own transl.) These enigmatic structures, which appear several times in the following account, could perhaps be identical with the prepared booths. Mathieu assumes, "Le mot doit désigner un 'espace vert' célèbre d'Héliopolis, peut-être attenant au temple de Rê" (72 n.190) and translates "le Parc". Fox is more reserved: "Some structure in the environs of the sanctuary. Neither the reading of the name nor its meaning is clear" (15 g.). For the reading, my suggestion is

$pr.w \ r3 \ / \ pr.w \ r3.w$ (twice singular, once plural). The meaning, though, remains unclear. $r3$ can be <u>utterance</u>, it can also mean <u>door, gate</u>; perhaps the latter meaning has to do with the celebrations around the yearly opening of the Ity-canal after the inundation.[5] Whatever the correct translation, the structures must be related to our topic, for the girl continues, "I went with you to the trees at the 'Houses-of-the-Gates' ", and finally we find her "My face directed to the <u>love garden</u>". The last expression is a Semitic word, doubtlessly related to the Hebrew root *dwd*, as explained by Fox (15 note m.).

Nature

The garden setting is indeed prominent in love lyrics probably all around the world. A digression to other Egyptian collections of love songs provides ample evidence. In the Turin Papyrus Cat. 1966 we read "Come, spend time where the young people are: the meadow celebrates its day. Under me are a festival booth and a hut." It is a sycamore tree in an orchard speaking here, and complaining: "She ... did not pour (a libation) for me, [on the d]ay of drinking, ... (I) was found useful (just) for amusement, [and was left] not drinking." The tree goddess, related in the sycamore to Hathor, the goddess of love, is offended by the lack of respect by the girl or the couple, who failed to libate water, surely because they were occupied with each other in a way the tree may now have in mind to disclose in revenge, when it threatens: "As my soul lives, O be-

---

[5] Fox 15 note c, quoting Ph. Derchain, Le Lotus, la mandragore et le perséa, *Chronique d'Égypte* 50, 1975, 83f.

loved one, you'll be paid back for this!" This must have been something better kept secret: "May she make you spend the day merrily, in a hut of reeds, in a guarded place" (translations by Fox, 45f.).

Nature as the setting brings to everyone's mind the Song of Songs (translations in the following by Fox). Here we find enclosed gardens, natural vegetation, cultivated fields, orchards and vineyards (Fox 285): "Come, my beloved, let's go to the field. We'll pass the night in the countryside; we'll go early to the vineyards." (Cant 7:12-13)

Although not explicitly mentioned in the Song of Songs, we may assume that the conspicuous watch towers in the vineyards (cf. Jes 1:8, 5:2) played a role in this context. Examples dating back to Biblical times can still be seen in significant numbers in the country, especially in the hills of Samaria, where they are called *manṭarah/manāṭir* by the Palestinian population. Gustaf Dalman recounts in his *Arbeit und Sitte in Palästina* that it was still customary in the early 20th century for the villagers to move and live in the towers or in tents erected on their tops, for the time of harvesting grapes. Girls and young women would then sit on the towers and sing a special genre of songs, called *imlālā*, which not surprisingly are dealing with love. Could *'et haz-zamīr*, "the time of song", in Cant 2:12 be related?[6]

Inside

In the Song of Songs it is the girl who assumes an active part: "I seized him - now I won't let him go till I've brought him to my mother's house, to the room of her who conceived me." (Cant 3:4). A rendezvous inside the home was a goal very hard to achieve, with such obstacles - moral and social norms set aside - as barred windows and shut doors: "Now he stands behind our wall, peering in through the windows, glancing in through the lattice." (Cant 2:9), "I slept, but my heart was awake. Listen! My lover is knocking: 'Open to me, my sister, my darling, ...' " (Cant 5:2, transl. New Standard Version). Compare the following passage from another collection of Egyptian love songs, Papyrus Chester Beatty I (no. 47): "I knocked, but it was not opened to me. ... Door, you are my fate! You are my (very) spirit." (transl. Fox). The distressed

---

[6] G. Dalman, *Arbeit und Sitte in Palästina*, Gütersloh 1928-1939 (2nd repr. 1987), I, 564ff., IV, 317f.

lover then promises sacrifices to the door's bolt, threshold, jambs and lintel, and finally wishes, the door would be of grass and the bolt of reeds.

Returning back to Papyrus Harris, promising prospects are held out in a passage hitherto not understood:

A 1 (1,2-3) "If you seek to embrace my hip, it is my <u>bedroom</u> that will receive you." (own transl.). *m p3jj=j mn[ḫb šsp]=f tj*

The suggested reconstruction of the lacuna is based on a comparison by Sarah Groll of the term *mnḫb*, lit. <u>cool room</u> (in private houses usually the sleeping room), with the "cool upper room", *ᶜaliyyat ham-mĕqerāh*, in Judges 3:20. Fox and Mathieu leave the second half of the sentence untranslated.

The happy end

What the couple in the above described situations would aspire, is an end to secrecy, and social acceptance of their relationship: "My brother was standing beside his mother, and with him all his kin. ... If only mother knew my heart - she would go inside for a while. <u>O Golden One</u>, put that in her heart! Then I could hurry to (my) brother and kiss him before his company, and not be ashamed because of anyone. I would be happy to have them see that you know me, and I'd hold festival to my goddess." (Pap. Chester Beatty I, no. 36; transl. Fox). This goddess, the "Golden One", is Hathor - and it becomes clear here that such fulfillment, the solution to the problems, is attributed to the divine powers. Love as a *Himmelsmacht*, a heavenly power, comes from God:

B 12 (5,2-3) "I have found, what <u>Amun</u> has given to me for eternity." (own transl.)

With the mentioning of Amun we are reminded of the beginning of this lecture, where there was talk of a <u>goose</u> - the sacred animal of this god. A goose is not a bird usually to be hunted and caught with baits. Obviously the goose is mentioned there in order to imply a desired intervention by Amun as cause of events. Its result then is described with simple but powerful expressions:

"The best has happened!" (B 13; 5,3) - "I am with you, I alone." (B 9; 4,5) - "May I never be far from your beauty!" (B 11; 4,11) - "You are in me and with me." (B 9; 4,6) - "My heart is in balance with your heart." (B 11; 4,11)

Stefan Wimmer

MATERNAL LOVE IN ANCIENT GREECE*

Did mothers in ancient Greece love their children? Your immediate response to this question may well be, "Of course they did!", for what could be more natural than a mother's instinct to nurture and love her offspring? Yet, in recent years, scholars have argued for a variety of reasons, that Greek mothers did not cherish their children in the same way that modern mothers do. In the words of a pathbreaking study of women in classical antiquity, Sarah Pomeroy's, *Goddesses, Whores, Wives, and Slaves*: "Mothers could not have been as attached to children as the ideal mother is nowadays." Pomeroy goes on to explain why this is so. Her first reason is related to the high infant mortality rate in ancient Greece. The majority of Greek mothers could expect to bury at least one child in their lifetime and this is thought to have conditioned maternal attitudes and led to a weakening of the emotional investment mothers would make in their children. Greek mothers, it is argued, had to blunt the force of their maternal feelings, if they were to preserve their own emotional equilibrium.[1] The hypothesis that Greek parents cared less about their children and did not mourn them quite so much when they died seems to be substantiated by several passages in Greek literature. In a notorious speech, Sophocles' Antigone, for example, explains that she is willing to defy Creon's edict and die in order to ensure Polyneices a proper burial, because Polyneices is her <u>brother</u>. If it were a question of a husband, Antigone contends, or a child, she would not behave in this way, for she could always marry again and have more children, but her brother is irreplaceable, now that Antigone's parents are dead (Sophocles *Antigone* 905-915). Children, it seems, can be replaced. We find similar arguments that children who will be born can serve as a substitute for progeny who have died - the claim "you can always have more children" - in Herodotus, Thucydides, and Euripides as well, and interestingly, such cold comfort is often put into the mouth of a woman.[2]

---

* This is the text of a paper delivered in Jerusalem in May 1998 at the "Art of Love Lyrics" conference. I have added notes and bibliography, but have made no attempt to change the informal tone of an oral presentation.

[1] Pomeroy 1975, 101. See also Golden 1990, 82-89; Garland 1990, 147-157.

[2] Herodotus 3. 119; Thucydides 2. 44.3; Euripides *Alcestis* 290-294 ; *Hypsipyle* fr. 60. 90-96. The authenticity of the passage in the *Antigone* is constantly debated - see

This is not to say, of course, that Greek mothers did not mourn their dead children. Women often played a prominent role in preparing the dead for burial and lamenting them, expressing their grief in ritual gestures and songs, and Greek myth provides instances of a whole series of mourning mothers. Niobe weeps over her dead children until she is turned to stone. Clytemnestra mourns her daughter Iphigenia and takes revenge upon her husband Agamemnon, who chose to sacrifice their daughter in order to ensure the success of his expedition to Troy. In an emotional passage in Euripides' *Trojan Women* (757-762), Andromache parts from her young son Astyanax who is about to be executed by his dead father's enemies. She bids farewell to the young child in her arms, mentioning the sweet scent of his skin (ὦ χρωτὸς ἡδὺ πνεῦμα 758). We are clearly meant to be moved by Andromache's feelings for her child and, indeed, the pitiable death of the infant Astyanax is a favorite subject in Athenian art from the 8th century BCE onwards, although his mother Andromache is not always part of the scene.[3]

One of the most poignant mothers found in Greek literature is the goddess Thetis, who mourns her son Achilles well before he actually dies. This *mater dolorosa* is the very first mother to be found in Greek literature, in Homer's *Iliad*. Thetis is married to a mortal, Peleus, and their son Achilles, the great Greek hero who fought at Troy, is mortal as well. Thus it is plain from the very start that Thetis will, of necessity, outlive her human son. Mother and son represent the unbridgeable gulf between the gods and human beings. And Achilles of the *Iliad* is more mortal than most, for the hero, despite his greatness and his goddess mother, is destined to be short-lived. He will die young, by his own choice, and while his actual demise is not included in the *Iliad*, Achilles' imminent death looms over great sections of the poem.[4] In a particularly dramatic scene, *Iliad* 18. 52-64, Thetis rushes to comfort her son Achilles, who lies prostrate on the ground, grieving for his dead friend Patroclus. The goddess is accompanied by her sisters, the Nereids, and she explains to these nymphs just how painful it is to be a mother. At first

---

e.g. the discussion and bibliography of Szlezák 1981. Beekes 1986 adduces parallels to this argument from other cultures.

[3] See Golden 1990, 89; Rühfel 1984, 45-58; *LIMC* i. 1, 767-774 and i. 2, 617-622 (Andromache I); ii. 1, 929-937 and ii. 2, 681-686 (Astyanax I).

[4] See e. g. Slatkin 1991, 34-40; Edwards 1991, 7-8.

she sounds like a proud mortal mother, telling her sisters how she has given birth to a mighty son, nurtured him, and seen him grow to powerful manhood. Yet Thetis is also an omniscient goddess, and she knows that her son will not return home from the fighting at Troy. Despite her divinity, she is unable to prevent her son's impending death, and she cannot even lighten his present burdens. "Yet while I see him live and he looks on the sunlight, he has/ sorrows, and though I go to him I can do nothing to help him."[5] Thetis' dual role as devoted mother and all-knowing deity is particularly fraught and that is why she speaks of δυσαριστοτόκεια (line 54), "the bitterness in this best of child-bearing." This unique triple compound, an oxymoron, was especially formulated by Homer for this passage in order to express Thetis' singular state.[6] The goddess' love for her mortal son makes her more vulnerable than most deities.

If in the *Iliad* Thetis is portrayed as a devoted, concerned mother, elsewhere she is painted in darker colors.[7] Hesiod tells us that she threw her children into a boiling cauldron, wishing to know if they were immortal. After several children had died, her husband Peleus stopped her, thus saving Achilles from a similar fate.[8] A mourning mother can, it seems, be a murderous mother and this is well exemplified by another famous figure in Greek myth, Medea. In Euripides' tragedy, Medea is rejected by her husband Jason, who decides to take a new wife, daughter of the ruler of Corinth. The vengeful Medea not only plots the death of Jason's new bride, but decides to kill her own two children as well, in order to punish their father. She is rent in two by her decision, and Euripides has her express her ambivalent feelings in a famous monologue (*Medea* 1019-1080). Medea speaks movingly of her two young sons and stresses the reciprocity of her bond with her children.[9] She bemoans the fact that she will not see her children grow up or attend their weddings.

---

[5] *Iliad* 18. 61-62 (R. Lattimore translation).

[6] See Edwards 1991, 151 (ad *Il.* 18. 54) on the "startling δυσαριστοτόκεια" and compare Garland 1990, 151.

[7] See Slatkin 1991 *passim* and Nagler 1996, esp. 149-151, on the darker sides of Thetis.

[8] Hesiod fr. 300 Merkelbach-West; cf. Apollodorus 4. 869 ff.

[9] See Gill 1996, 166-174. The recent collection Clauss and Johnston 1997, illuminates the character of Medea in Euripides (and elsewhere) from a variety of perspectives.

Nor will she, their mother, be supported by them in her old age (1025-1028, 1032-1035). Medea dwells upon her children's physical beauty, their soft skin and sweet breath (ὦ μαλθακὸς χρὼς πνεῦμά θ' ἥδιστον τέκνων 1075), and we have already seen that another mother in a later play by Euripides, Andromache, echoes this detail when bidding farewell to her young child.[10] Andromache's son is torn from her and killed by her enemies, while it is Medea who will execute her own children, but both mothers express their maternal love in virtually identical fashion. How should we understand the parallels between these two tragic mothers? Does Andromache echo Medea's words simply because Euripides chose to employ once again a telling physical detail to great dramatic effect? Or should we understand that Medea is no less sincere than the bereaved Andromache? What are we to make of a mourning, murderous mother, such as Medea? It is perhaps salutary to remember at this point that Medea's words were written by a man, spoken by a male actor, and performed in front of a large Athenian audience which may - but on the other hand may not - have included women. Ancient evidence for the presence of women at the performance of Greek tragedies is contradictory and inconclusive and we do not know if real-life Greek mothers actually had the opportunity to hear and react to Medea.[11] I would like to stress the gap between the violent mothers of myth and actual Greek women because there may have been little relation between the feelings and attitudes of these two groups of women. In recent years, much interesting work has been done on the role attributed to women - by men - in Greek tragedy. The women of tragedy are often assigned radical, powerful and destructive deeds, very unlike the everyday domestic ones of ordinary Athenian women. These dramatic figures are used to examine and expose underlying tensions in Greek society, tensions concerning gender roles and relating to the conflict between oikos and polis, between the private sphere and the public sphere.[12] Medea, in other words, cannot simply be taken as a representative Greek mother.

I turn now to what is probably the most problematical aspect of Greek maternal behavior, the widespread use of exposure as a means of

---

[10] Compare also *Medea* 1030 with *Troades* 760.

[11] Goldhill 1997, 61-66 is a recent discussion with further references.

[12] See Gould 1980; Blundell 1995, 172-180; Zeitlin 1996.

family planning.[13] An unwanted infant was exposed immediately after birth, abandoned in some secluded spot and left to die, or, at best, placed in a public place where passersby - a childless couple or a slave dealer, for instance - might conceivably take the child home and raise it. The Greeks did not actually kill unwanted newborns, apparently because that would lead to pollution by bloodguilt. Exposure, then, is not quite infanticide. Indeed the Greeks themselves carefully distinguish in language and practice between the exposure of a newborn baby and the killing of a young child who was a recognized and named member of a family.[14] Only the latter practice was prohibited by law and condemned by society. I need hardly say that modern sensibilities find the practice of exposure incomprehensible and abhorrent and, in the words of one commentator, "the apparent acceptance by certain Greeks of this practice is arguably what separates us most radically from their mentality."[15] Indeed the gap is so great that some modern scholars try to excuse, deny, or explain away the unsavory custom of abandoning newborn children.[16]

How common was the practice of exposure and what part did mothers play in determining the fate of their children? Neither of these questions is easy to answer. Evidence for the exposure of children in early Greece is chiefly literary. You are all familiar with the most famous exposed child of all, Oedipus, who was saved by a kind-hearted shepherd, only to go on to fulfill the cruel destiny allotted to him by the gods. Exposed children who are subsequently adopted are frequently a pivotal part of the plot in plays by Menander and other writers of New Comedy. These literary references to exposure need not reflect real-life practices, but most scholars are agreed that exposure or infanticide of legitimate offspring, particularly of daughters was not unknown in classical Athens, for example, and it _may_ even have been a fairly common practice.[17] Girls, it seems, were abandoned more frequently than boys,

---

[13] Eyben 1980-1981 is a detailed and useful survey. Patterson 1985 is the most thoughtful of a series of recent articles and examines earlier work.

[14] See Patterson 1985, esp. 106-107 and 112 and Golden 1981, 330-331 on the use of ἐκτίθημι, ἐκβάλλω and βρέφος (for the exposure of newborn children) vs. παιδοκτονέω the killing of a young child.

[15] Garland 1990, 85.

[16] Engels 1980, 112-130, is an outstanding instance. See Harris 1982; Golden 1990, 86-89; and the arguments from silence used by Lacey 1968, 165-166.

[17] See Golden 1981; Eyben 1980-1981, 13-14 with n. 31.

both because they were a greater burden financially and because they were simply valued less. In a letter written on papyrus dating from the first century BCE, a Greek soldier writes to his wife (*P. Oxy.* 4. 744): "If you happen to give birth, if it is a boy let it be, but if it is a girl cast it out." (ἐὰν ἦ ἄρσενον, ἄφες. ἐὰν ἦν θήλεα, ἔκβαλε.) This paternal attitude is countered by the practice attributed to those imaginary women warriors, the Amazons. Amazons, who lead a life which is the very opposite of that of ordinary Greek women, are said to keep their girl children and kill, maim, or send away the boys for adoption.[18] In the case of the fictitious Amazons, it is the mother who decides what is to be done with newborns, but in Athens and the majority of Greek cities, fathers had the final power of decision, for children legally belonged to their fathers. Such paternal domination is in fact the second reason given by Sarah Pomeroy for thinking that Greek mothers were less attached to their offspring than their modern counterparts.[19] Legally, then, mothers had to bow to patriarchal authority when it came to deciding the fate of their newborn children, but what happened in practice? How did mothers feel about exposing their children? Were they consulted by their husbands and a party to the decision about rearing a child? Here too we must turn to literature for hints of women's attitudes. In a justly famous passage of Plato's dialogue *Theaetetus*, Socrates describes himself as a midwife of sorts, someone who helps brings to fruition and life not children, but the ideas and mental conceptions of others. Some ideas, like some children, are weak and Socrates warns his fellow conversationalist Theaetetus that if he steals away with such mental offspring and abandons them, Theaetetus is not to behave savagely, as do mothers with their first-born children (μὴ ἀγρίαινε ὥσπερ αἱ πρωτοτόκοι περὶ τὰ παιδία *Theaetetus* 151c; cf. 161a). This reference to the fury of mothers whose first-born infants are exposed is noteworthy precisely because it is so casual. It is a truism for Plato and his readers that mothers do not give up their children lightly. Or, to be more precise, their first-born children. It is thought that eldest children, but not necessarily younger

---

[18] Kill male infants: Hellanicus *FGrH* 4 F 167c; Maim: Hippocrates, *De Articulis* (53, Littré iv. 232); Diodorus Siculus 2. 45. 3; Send away: Strabo 11. 5. 1. On the Amazons in general see e. g. Fantham *et al.* 1994, 128-135 and the further references there.

[19] Pomeroy 1975, 101.

ones, were generally kept and raised[20] and that may be why their mothers are passionately angry when such children are abandoned, even if they are weak and sickly. It may have been more customary to expose a second, third, or fourth child and perhaps, with these later births, women became more resigned and learned to reconcile themselves to the cruel practice.

In his play *Ion*, Euripides presents us with the thoughts and feelings of a mother who has exposed her child on her own initiative. The work is a curious blend of the light and the dark, a serio-comic tragedy, as it were, and the mother here, Creusa, is no Medea, but an engaging and sympathetic figure. Creusa is an Athenian princess who has been raped by the god Apollo, and then gives birth to a son, Ion, whom she exposes. The child, unbeknown to her, is rescued through the devices of his divine father and grows up in Delphi. Some 18 years later, mother and son are re-united at Delphi, after a series of misunderstandings. That Creusa has abandoned her child and believes him dead is an important part of the play's workings, but Euripides seems to stress this fact above and beyond the needs of the plot. The actual act of exposure - the way Creusa took her newborn son, placed him in a basket with birth tokens, and left him in the cave where Apollo had raped her - is described no less than five times.[21] We also see the act of exposure from several different perspectives. Creusa imagines that the baby has been killed by wild beasts or preyed upon by birds, dwelling upon these horrible pictures several times.[22] We, the audience, know from the start that her son Ion has survived and Euripides probably lingers on such gory images for dramatic effect, vividly portraying the guilt felt by a mother who has exposed her child. But the tragedian may also be interested in having his audience contend with reality and confront the cruel physical fate of abandoned children. Exposed children, after all, were not found only in the realm of myth.[23] When Creusa tells her old trusted servant about exposing her son, breaking the silence of many years, the old man makes it plain that he is horrified by her deed (*Ion* 951-963). Euripides, I think,

---

[20] See Lacey 1968, 164.

[21] Euripides *Ion* 10-27, 338-354, 887-918, 931-965, 1472-1499.

[22] Euripides *Ion* 348-352, 503-505, 903, 917, 933, 951.

[23] See Garland 1990, 91; Lee 1997, 267 (ad *Ion* 954).

uses dialogue here, rather than having Creusa simply tell her tale in a set speech, so that we will notice the old servant's reactions as well. The old man is disturbed by the fact that Creusa has exposed her baby by herself, for normally - in literature and probably in life - a servant was used for such a forbidding task, and he seems genuinely disturbed by the morality of her action. "How could you bring yourself to do it?" the old servant asks Creusa (line 958) and he condemns her for her hard heart (line 960). The old man uses three cognate Greek words here - ἔτλης, τλήμων and τόλμης - to describe Creusa's deed, and these words can be taken either actively in the sense of "to dare, to act heartlessly" or passively, "to suffer, endure."[24] If the servant sees Creusa as harsh and daring, she perceives herself as a wretched victim forced to endure. In this exchange, Creusa makes it plain that she has returned to the scene in her mind again and again, re-creating and recasting the actual circumstances of the exposure. Thus she imagines the newborn baby stretching its hands towards her, the behavior of a much older child, and this makes her rejection of him all the more painful. Were there any mothers - or for that matter, fathers - sitting in the audience who had undergone a similar trauma? Drama is not, of course, documentary evidence and I think that Robert Garland goes too far when he argues on the basis of the *Ion* that "Euripides regarded the practice of exposure with repugnance and horror."[25] Yet Garland may well be right in using the play as evidence that the morality of exposing children was called into question in late 5th and early 4th century Athens.

Turning to Sparta, we find that it is neither the father nor the mother who determined whether a child was to be exposed, but representatives of the state, elders of the tribes. Soon after birth, infant boys were brought by their fathers to be inspected by the elders. Well-formed, healthy children were to be raised, while ill-born, unshapely ones had to be exposed at a special spot. It was illegal for parents to rear their baby without permission and there was no room for the hope (or illusion) that others would take up these abandoned children. Plutarch (*Lycurgus* 16. 1-2) is our source for this regulation and his language - he consistently uses the neuter gender to describe the newly-born infants - does not al-

---

[24] See Lee 1997, 188 (ad *Ion* 252-254) and 267 (ad 960).
[25] Garland 1990, 91.

low us to determine whether baby girls were inspected as well. It is possible that the decision about raising female infants was left to the parents[26] and here too we do not know what part the mother played in such decisions. Spartan women, while seen primarily as mothers of future warriors, were allowed a certain amount of freedom in comparison with their Athenian counterparts. They had considerable authority in deciding internal domestic matters, partly because their husbands spent much time away from home in communal barracks or on military campaigns.[27] Spartan mothers are, of course, notorious for their willingness, even eagerness, to sacrifice their sons on the battlefield. You are probably familiar with the story of the strong-minded Spartan mother who hands her son his shield as he is about to depart for battle and laconically, but bluntly states: "Either on this or with this." This is one of a series of anecdotes on tough Spartan women reproduced by the 1st-2nd century CE writer Plutarch (*Moralia* 241f) and it is difficult to determine just how authentic such traditions are. If Spartan women do not seem to demonstrate a great deal of maternal love towards their sons, the dearth of evidence, anecdotal or otherwise, about Spartan mothers and daughters leaves us free to conjecture more positive relations. One recent scholar paints a rosy picture of intimate mother-daughter relationships, conducted in a virtually male-less household, with both generations of women enjoying considerable independence and activity outside the home.[28] Perhaps this was so.

Let us turn to what seems to be an actual mother-daughter relationship in archaic Lesbos at the beginning of the 6th century BCE. Virtually all of surviving Greek literature was written by men, and this makes our last text, a fragmentary poem addressed by the early female poet Sappho to her daughter Cleis, all the more valuable. This poem (Sappho fr. 132), a truncated love lyric, if you will, is not without its difficulties. We have, for a start, only three lines of what could have been a much longer and more complex work. There are also those who argue that the ancient biographical tradition which states that Cleis was Sappho's daughter is unreliable and the word παῖς in the poem should be

---

[26] MacDowell 1986, 52-53 and 71; see too Huys 1996.

[27] See e.g. Blundell 1995, 150-158; Fantham *et al.* 1994, 56-67; Cartledge 1981.

[28] Blundell 1995, 151-152.

understood as young girl or even slave, rather than daughter.[29] So too a poet's or poetess' lyrical persona need not reflect their actual self. Let us look nonetheless at this brief celebration of maternal love. Sappho compares her beautiful daughter to golden flowers - such flower imagery is frequently found in her poems - and declares that she would not exchange her beloved child for all the wealth and power, luxury and might symbolized by the great kingdom of Lydia. Sappho pretends that Kleis is a commodity in an imaginary market place, only in order to reject the idea of trading in her treasure. She values her daughter above all.[30] One word found in this fragment - ἀγαπάτα - beloved, is particularly interesting, for Sappho is apparently the first writer to use this word of a daughter. Before Sappho, the adjective in its masculine form, ἀγαπητός, was used only in relation to male only children, children such as Hector and Andromache's son Astyanax, who are their parents' heirs and sole hope for the future. Sappho now applies this word to <u>her</u> only child, <u>her</u> hope for the future, her daughter Cleis.[31] These three lines are, I think, genuine love lyrics, an authentic expression of maternal love, written by an actual mother.

* * *

When all is said and done, how can we measure the depth and dimension of maternal feelings in ancient Greece? There is documentary evidence, of sorts, for the attitudes of Greek mothers, such as the epigraphic records of women who make dedications to the gods on behalf of their sick children. There are also children's tombstones which make mention of their loving mothers, but we know that in various times and places it was the practice to omit mothers' names and include only fathers on epitaphs.[32] One could also argue that the sentiments written on tombstones are more conventional than real, even if the very conventions teach us something about a society's values and mores. We can also look at artistic representations of mothers and their children, even if

---

[29] Thus, for instance, Burnett 1983, 279 with n. 2.

[30] See Burnett 1983, 279 and Blundell 1995, 86 and compare Sappho fr. 16.

[31] See the excellent discussion of Hallett 1982.

[32] See Lefkowitz and Fant 1992, nos. 274-275 with p. 350 n. 82; cf. Golden 1990, 189-190 n. 6; Fantham et al. 1994, 5-8, 81-83.

these representations, too, may reflect conventions, rather than reality.[33] I could quote to you the pronouncements of Xenophon and Aristotle on the force of maternal love.[34] I could also present to you many more instances of unloving mothers in Greek myth and literature, women who mistreated their children in one fashion or another. Helen leaves her small daughter behind when she goes off to Troy, Praxithea willingly sacrifices her daughter to save her city, Procne cuts up her son to bits and feeds him to her husband etc. etc. And there are, of course, many more loving mythical mothers as well, most notably Demeter who grieves for her abducted daughter Persephone so much that she upsets the natural order of the world until her daughter is restored to her. Yet women of Greek myth and literature are not representations of real women and are not meant to be so, and we must use literary texts very carefully in any attempt to trace the attitudes of actual Greek mothers.

Did Greek mothers love their children? Clearly different cultures - and different individuals within various societies - use different means to express their emotions. Greeks - and Greek mothers - are not us.[35] We can if we choose stress the evidence pointing to the negative aspects of Greek motherhood and assume that maternal love in ancient Greece was deficient or lacking, and that the Greeks were vastly different from us in their attitudes towards children. The words of the poet and classics professor, Louis MacNeice, are a particularly apt expression of this approach to the Greeks as essentially foreign to us.

> And how one can imagine oneself among them
>> I do not know
> It was all so unimaginably different
>> And all so long ago.[36]

---

[33] Rühfel 1984 surveys the portrayal of children in Greek art; Ridgway 1987 is an interesting discussion of ancient Greek women and their relationship to the visual arts, as sponsors as well as objects. Cf. also Bonfante 1997.

[34] Aristotle tells us that parents and particularly mothers love their children (*Ethica Nicomachea* 1161 b17-27; cf. 1168 a21-26). Xenophon (*Memorabilia* 2. 2. 5) emphasizes the mother's role in conceiving, carrying, bearing, and nurturing children. Xenophon also notes that women are granted by the gods more affection towards newborn babies than men are (*Oeconomicus* 7. 24).

[35] See the thoughtful discussion of Golden 1988, esp. 159-160.

[36] MacNeice 1949, 139 ("Autumn Journal" ix); cf. Knox 1993, esp. 25-31, 63-67.

On the other hand, there is so much in Greek culture which speaks directly and vibrantly to us across the centuries that it is difficult to conceive of Greek mothers as being such alien creatures. We must not gloss over unpleasant facts such as the exposure of children, nor should we forget that virtually all the testimony relating to maternal love in Greece comes filtered through the perceptions and works of men. While it is clearly wrong simply to ascribe our values, thoughts, and sentiments to the Greeks, it seems equally misguided to believe that maternal feelings have drastically altered over the centuries.

Deborah Levine Gera

Bibliography

Beekes, R. S. P. (1986). "«You Can Get New Children...»: Turkish and other parallels to ancient Greek ideas in Herodotus, Thucydides, Sophocles and Euripides." *Mnemosyne* 39: 225-239.

Blundell, S. (1995). *Women in Ancient Greece*. Cambridge, Massachusetts.

Bonfante, L. (1997). "Nursing Mothers in Classical Art." *Naked Truths: Women, sexuality and gender*. Eds. A. O. Koloski-Ostrov and C. L. Lyons. London, 174-186.

Burnett, A. P. (1983). *Three Archaic Poets: Archilochus, Alcaeus, Sappho*. London.

Cartledge, P. (1981). "Spartan Wives: Liberation or License?" *Classical Quarterly* 31: 84-105.

Clauss, J. J. and S. I. Johnston, Eds. (1997). *Medea: Essays on Medea in Myth, Literature, Philosophy, and Art*. Princeton.

Edwards, M. W. (1991). *The Iliad: A Commentary: Volume V: Books 17-20*. Cambridge.

Engels, D. (1980). "The Problem of Female Infanticide in the Greco-Roman World." *Classical Philology* 75: 112-130.

Eyben, E. (1980-1981). "Family Planning in Graeco-Roman Antiquity." *Ancient Society* 11-12: 5-82.

Fantham, E. et al., Eds. (1994). *Women in the Classical World*. New York and Oxford.

Garland, R. (1990). *The Greek Way of Life*. London.

Gill, C. (1996). *Personality in Greek, Epic, Tragedy, and Philosophy*. Oxford.

Golden, M. (1981). "Demography and the Exposure of Girls at Athens." *Phoenix* 35: 316-331.

Golden, M. (1988). "Did the Ancients Care When Their Children Died?" *Greece and Rome* 35: 152-163.

Golden, M. (1990). *Children and Childhood in Classical Athens*. Baltimore.

Goldhill, S. (1997). "The audience of Athenian tragedy." *The Cambridge Companion to Greek Tragedy*. Ed. P. E. Easterling. Cambridge, 54-68.

Gould, J. (1980). "Law, Custom and Myth: Aspects of the Social Position of Women in Classical Athens." *Journal of Hellenic Studies* 100: 38-59.

Hallett, J. P. (1982). "Beloved Cleis." *Quaderni urbinati di cultura classica* 10: 21-31.

Harris, W. V. (1982). "The Theoretical Possibility of Extensive Infanticide in the Greco-Roman World." *Classical Quarterly* 32: 114-116.

Huys, M. (1996). "Spartan Practice of Selective Infanticide and its Parallels in Ancient Utopian Tradition." *Ancient Society* 27: 47-74.

Knox, B. (1993). *The Oldest Dead White European Males*. New York.

Lacey, W. K. (1968). *The Family in Classical Greece*. Ithaca, New York.

Lee, K. H. (1997). *Euripides, Ion*. Warminster.

Lefkowitz, M. R. and M. B. Fant (1992). *Women's Life in Greece and Rome*. 2nd ed. London.

LIMC (1981-1984). *Lexicon Iconographicum Mythologiae Classicae*. Zurich and Munich.

MacDowell, D. M. (1986). *Spartan Law*. Edinburgh.

MacNeice, L. (1949). *Collected Poems*. London.

Nagler, M. N. (1996). "Dread Goddess Revisited." *Reading the Odyssey*. Ed. S. L. Schein. Princeton, 141-161.

Patterson, C. (1985). "Not Worth the Rearing: The Causes of Infant Exposure in Ancient Greece." *Transactions of the American Philological Association* 115: 103-123.

Pomeroy, S. B. (1975). *Goddesses, Whores, Wives, and Slaves*. New York.

Ridgway, B. S. (1987). "Ancient Greek Women and Art: The Material Evidence." *American Journal of Archaeology* 91: 399-409.

Rühfel, H. (1984). *Das Kind in der griechischen Kunst*. Mainz.

Slatkin, L. M. (1991). *The Power of Thetis*. Berkeley.

Szlezák, T. A. (1981). "Bemerkungen zur Diskussion um Sophokles, Antigone 904-920." *Rheinisches Museum für Philologie* 124: 108-142.

Zeitlin, F. I. (1996). "Playing the Other: theater, theatricality and the feminine in Greek drama." *Playing the Other. Gender and Society in Classical Greek Literature*. Chicago, 341-374.

"LOVE YOUR NEIGHBOR"
IN LEVITICUS 19 AND IN ANCIENT EGYPTIAN

In reflecting on the "Love your neighbor" command in Leviticus chapter 19, one needs to read all of verses 17 and 18 together in order to obtain the precise meaning; and one must also read verse 34 of chapter 19. I now read the three verses to you in the rendering of the Revised Standard Version:

(17) You shall not hate your brother in your heart,

but you shall reason with your neighbor,

lest you bear sin because of him.

(18) You shall not take vengeance or bear any grudge against the sons of your own people, but you shall love your neighbor as yourself. I am the Lord.

(34) The stranger who sojourns with you shall be to you as the native among you, and you shall love him as yourself; for you were stranger in the land of Egypt. I am the Lord your God.

The Hebrew words for "your brother" and "your neighbor" in verse 17 are *aḥikha* and *'amitekha*; and it is clear from the context that the two terms refer to the same kind of persons, namely, neither to your blood-brother, nor to your next-door neighbor, but rather to all your fellow human beings in the community of Israel, people with whom you may reason, but whom you may not hate but should love.

The Egyptian saying that I shall now compare is found in Papyrus Chester Beatty No. IV, which was published along with all the other Chester Beatty Papyri in Sir Alan Gardiner's edition entitled *Hieratic Papyri in the British Museum, Third Series: Chester Beatty Gift* (London 1935). The date of P. Chester Beatty No. IV is Ramesside. The *recto* of P. Chester Beatty No. IV contains two long hymns to the sun-god Amun-Re, praising him as creator of mankind and all other creatures. The *verso* of the papyrus has a miscellany of instructional texts. One section of it is often cited by Egyptologists because it recalls by name eight famous scribes of the past whose tombs are lost and forgotten, but whose written works keep their names alive. The other parts of the Miscellany have been rather neglected. It is likely that the scribe of P. Chester Beatty IV had assembled, or was copying an assemblage of, individual instructions which were broken fragments of what once had been a unified instructional work. I have cited four of these brief miscellaneous instructions in my last book - *Moral Values in Ancient Egypt* (1997). The fourth of the sayings cited there is the equivalent of the biblical "Love your neighbor" command. I now cite it in my English translation and in the Egyptian wording:

> Do not sit before your superior,
> Respect another, that you be respected,
> Love people, then people love you!
> *m-ir ḥms m-bȝḥ, ꜥȝ r.k*
> *tri ky tri.tw.k*
> *mry rmṯ mry tw rmṯ*
> (P.Chester Beatty IV verso 4,6-7).

The remarkable similarity between the Egyptian and the biblical commands results from shared attitudes and from the wording itself. As to shared attitudes, both nations recognized differences in rank, but nevertheless viewed human beings as basically equal members of a close-knit community. Just as *aḥikha* and *'amitekha* meant your fellowmen-and-women in your society, so Egyptian *rmṯ*, written with male and female determinative and plural strokes, meant "people", even though Gardiner translated the sentence as "Love men, that men may love thee."

The second shared attitude is the notion of reciprocal action. And here we find that both sayings limit reciprocal action to the doing of good and exclude revenge. The biblical command forbids revenge explicitly - "You shall not hate your brother" etc. The Egyptian saying implies the rejection of revenge. The explicit rejection of revenge is formulated quite early and quite often in Egyptian autobiographies and in the instructional texts. I cite here just two examples from the autobiographies.

(1) The nomarch Kheti of Siut, tomb no. 4, declared:

> I turned my back on the lover of lies,
> I judged not one innocent by another's charge,
> I answered evil with good.

(2) A thousand years later, the fourth prophet of Amun Djedkhonsefankh (statue Cairo 559) declared:

> I kept my mouth clean of harming him who harmed me,
> My benevolence turned my foes into my friends.

Conciliation was the keynote of Egyptian ethics; and conciliation was also the guiding principle of civil law. A judge hearing the case of two contending parties did not aim at imposing a judgment; rather, he aimed at getting the two parties to work out a compromise acceptable to both. And the "Instructions", notably those of Any and Amenemope, had a great deal to say about shunning vengeance and leaving retribution to the gods. The Egyptians firmly believed that the gods watched over the functioning of *Maat*, the right order of all life which they had created, and which entailed the principle that doing right brought success in life, while evildoing inevitably brought failure. This optimism about the goodness of life was reiterated in the literary texts for more than two millennia. And this optimism is one of the principal traits that makes ancient Egyptian culture so very different from the culture of ancient Greece. In the Greek character there was a large measure of pessimism and of combativeness, wherefore reciprocation in its dual forms of loving one's friends and hating one's enemies prevailed in Greece for many centuries, until the principle of revenge was overcome and set aside during the fifth century B.C. and thereafter.

In addition to the shared sense of communal interdependence, and of reciprocation as its mechanism, the similarity between the biblical and the Egyptian commands rests most of all on the use of the verb "love." I have quoted the nomarch Kheti of Siut, who declared "I answered evil with good". I now quote from the same inscription at the front of his tomb:

I have come from my town,

I have descended from my nome,

having done what people love and gods praise.

I have given bread to the hungry, clothes to the naked,

I listened to the plea of the widow,

I gave a home to the orphan.

If you add the ever repeated affirmation of love of family:

I am the beloved of his father,

the praised of his mother,

loved by his siblings,

kind to his kindred (Schenkel, MHT, no.241)

you have the central values of Egyptian ethics in early formulations around 2000 B.C. In the following two millennia the same basic values, and additional ones, are repeated with more refinement and sophistication. And so I came across the formulation of P. Chester Beatty IV, "Love people that people may love you," written down in the Ramesside age, i.e. 1300-1100 B.C.

Then I encountered a questioner in the person of Prof. Abraham Malamat, who contributed to the Festschrift for Prof. Rolf Rendtorff an article entitled: "You shall love your neighbor as yourself - a case of misinterpretation?" In this article Malamat asked whether *ve-ahavta le-re'akha kamokha* might not mean "Be useful, or helpful to your neighbor as to yourself"? He supported the suggestion by citing biblical passages in which the verb *ahav* suggests the meaning of "usage" rather than of "love." His final example is 2 Chr. 26:10, where king Uzziah is said to have been "*ohev adamah*" - the full sentence is *ki ohev adamah hayah* - ; and Malamat remarked that renderings like the king "was a lover of the soil" are too modern and anachronistic. I want to answer his question by making two interrelated points. One is that both biblical *ahav* and Egyptian *mri* were verbs the meanings of which extended beyond the core sense of "love." And that is due to the fact that the vocabulary of these two ancient languages was much smaller than that of modern languages, wherefore individual lexemes often had wider ranges of meaning than ours do. Secondly, even in our languages, the verb "love" has a wide range of usages. For instance, I "love" my garden; and my garden depends for its well-being on my "loving care." And any dog owner might tell you that he "loves" his dog. Then there is the aesthetic dimension: we "love" music etc. Thus, in sum, the notion of "being useful/helpful" to your neighbor is quite naturally included in the "love your neighbor" formulation. And it is precisely the use of the terms for "love" in the biblical and the Egyptian commands, and their being directed to the communities as a whole, that makes the two sayings practically identical.

What prevents the two teachings from being fully identical is that biblical "Love your neighbor" is formulated as a divine command and thus an absolute one, whereas Egyptian moral instructions do not claim divine origin or inspiration. Egyptian gods did not speak to man or woman except on rare and specific occasions. Queen Hatshepsut recorded that her divine father, the god Amun, had spoken to her and advised her to undertake the expedition to Punt (Urk. IV. 342ff.). Nonroyal persons, man or woman, never claimed that a god or goddess had spoken to them except when they told of a dream in which a god or goddess had appeared to them and had advised them on a particular practical matter that concerned them. But though the gods were not viewed as teachers of mankind, they were viewed as creators of all that exists, who watched over their creation and who guided mankind as shepherds. I now read to you just two quatrains from one of the two great hymns to the creator-god which is written on the *recto* of P. Chester Beatty IV. The creator-god is addressed by a four-fold name:

> Praise to you, Amun-Re-Atum-Harakhti,
> by whose words beings began,
> mankind, gods, cattle, game of all kinds,
> and all that flies and alights!

> Valiant herdsman herding them ever!
> Bodies are filled with your goodness.
> Eyes behold through you, all are in awe of you,
> their hearts turned to you.

Here, in the Ramesside age, Egyptian moral and religious thinking reached its most advanced and mature stage. The four-fold name of the creator-god - Amun-Re-Atum-Harakhti - signifies that, behind the different names and forms of appearance, the divine was an encompassing unity. And this divinity that had made everything was the herds-man of mankind.

In daily practice, naturally, people would pray to their local gods; and we know a great many of these prayers. But I here mention hymns and prayers only as background to our examination of the "love your neighbor" saying as found in P. Chester Beatty IV, *verso*. We found it there on page 4 of the Miscellany of moral instructions that occupies the entire *verso*. Two pages earlier, on *verso* 2,4-5 there occurs the following instruction:

> As for the man whom his god has built up,
> he should nourish many!

ir s ḳd sw nṯr.f ḥr sᶜnḫ.n.f ḳnw
(P. Chaster Beatty IV *verso* 2, 4-5)

That means, a man who, by the favor of the god whom he worships, is wealthy and well placed, should help many less fortunate people.

When I first read this saying I was struck by the thought that this one-sentence instruction is a concrete description of the concept of *philanthropia* as developed centuries later in Greece, about which one can read an excellent chapter in John Ferguson's *Moral Values in the Ancient World* (London 1958).

In conclusion, I shall repeat the "love people" teaching of P. Chester Beatty IV *verso* 4,6-7 and add to it the teaching of *verso* 2,4-5:

Do not sit before your superior,

Respect another, that you be respected,

Love people, then people love you.

As for the man whom his god has built up,

he should nourish many!

I believe that these five lines closely match the wording and the spirit of Leviticus 19,17-18v, with that difference that the biblical version is a divine command, whereas the Egyptian teaching reflects the morality of an advanced polytheism in which the gods were the creators and benefactors, but not the teachers, of mankind.

Miriam Lichtheim

LOVE AS POLITICAL POWER

In this paper I would like to emphasize the role and value of new trends which occur in the Egyptian society during the El-Amarna period, and which portray the antagonism between individualism and social collective patterns. I would like to trace the departure from the clan or community to individualism within the community. This phenomenon is well illustrated when one examines the function of love in the El-Amarna theology.

The El-Amarna regime actually resembles a kind of community which is governed by the king, who is a teacher of an elite. This elite studies and functions as a collective study-group, the head of which is the king, who has love bestowed upon him by the 'one god'. Akhenaten's disciples demonstrate the sense of 'Truth' - they declare themselves to operate according to the principles of 'Truth and Justice', in the following manner:

1) They know that their awareness of the king's existence is based upon the king's utter attachment to justice, or in their words: "I did justice/truth because I know that the king survives because of truth" (Sandman 1938, p. 76, lines 13-14, 15-16).

The disciples do not claim to act according to principles of truth/justice because they are morally and intellectually convinced that these are the 'right' principles of conduct, nor do they thus behave owing to a command being given to act according to 'the Truth'. They keep on stressing their behavior as being in accordance with the principles of 'truth and justice' <u>as a direct result of their wanting to please the king personally</u>. This is a personal relationship between a disciple - a pupil - and his teacher. The disciples are convinced that this is the right way because <u>they love their teacher</u> (Sandman 1938, p. 76, line 8).

2) The behavior of the disciples according to principles of truth and justice makes the king happy; or to put it differently - they know that falsehood is detested by the king.

3) Also, the principles of truth and justice run in their blood, these principles are in their belly (Sandman 1938, p. 77, line 4). Truth/Justice has become an instinct, deeply rooted. As a result of discussion or conversation with the king his disciples have developed instincts for the truth. The wonder of the king has become a natural part of them. This is

an internalization of the theory of Athenism, namely the king's charisma 'bi 3t' as a teacher and spiritual leader, as a philosopher - his ability to cause them to want to please him, to make him happy and even to imitate him - all these merge into one entity and are manifested in their behavior with concordance to principles of truth and justice which symbolize him.

This merging process is much emphasized in the love songs. The El-Amarna theology does not compel its followers to obey an apodictic system of commandments (such as "do not steal" or "do not murder"), because the El-Amarna philosophy does not want to enter from outside. This is a pedagogic philosophy of educating people from the inside, this is a theology of within, and it attempts to shape men from within.

Men most feel love, they have to be excited, think and understand and as a result, fulfill truth and justice. It is the instinct or impulse for truth which is accomplished as a product of an educational process - philosophical thinking and contemplation - which is done with a divine teacher. In this manner, moral knowledge and superiority belong to the philosophical elite of El-Amarna.

Since the whole depends upon its parts, the parts have to be unique. They have to define themselves as uniquely meaningful and valuable. They have to be uniquely singularized yet they have to act in mutual understanding of each other as well as of the theology of El-Amarna.

One phrase is repeated frequently in the theology of El-Amarna: the king knows how to raise the 'd3mw' (young) as 'd3mw'. The king educates the second generation - his 'young followers' - according to the 'young character'. This is the highest attribute of Akhenaten.

Thus the political and cultural elite in the El-Amarna period was educated individually and not as part of a compulsive regime. The structure of the regime can be described as follows:

God Athen loves the king (Sandman 1938, pp. 59, line 10; 75, lines 10, 13; 91, line 2)

The king loves truth (Sandman 1938, p. 76, line 13)

The disciples love the king and truth (Sandman 1938, p. 77, line 2)

Love is the common denominator, or essential force, which unites the subjects of the regime unto a homogenous community.

Each of the grave owners considered himself special while trying to please the king. They all wanted to become his image. God loves his creatures (Sandman 1938, p. 76, lines 2-3) - not a sexual love, but a love which expresses intellectual identity. The basis for love is the solar energy which warms everything - it is the element which holds together the intellectual and spiritual life.

Bibliography:
Hornung, E. 1983. *Conceptions of God in Ancient Egypt: The One and the Many.* London.
Sandman M. 1938. *Texts from the Time of Akhenaten.* Bruxelles.

Sara I. Groll

LOVE IN COPTIC MONASTIC TRADITION

Two polarities of human being

It is well known that from the beginning of the Christian era, love became a special sign of the followers of Christ, for Jesus himself recommended it to his disciples (ex. John 13:34-35). On the one hand, Christianity has never rejected sexual love between woman and man, but on the other, it has constantly proposed a new form of life, that of purity and virginity. This found a particular expression in a solitary way of living common in the Middle East (Egypt, Palestine, Syria) from the fourth century onward. How did these people understand human nature with its two polarities: that of man and that of woman, with love between the two as an essential element for human existence?

The first chapter of the *Book of Genesis* (Gen 1:26-27) says that God made man (ἄνθρωπον) in his image and after his likeness (κατ᾽ εἰκόνα ἡμετέραν καὶ καθ᾽ ὁμοίωσιν) and explains that this finds its expression in the bi-polarity of male and female: "So God created man (τὸν ἄνθρωπον) in his own image, in the image of God (κατ᾽ εἰκόνα θεοῦ) he created him; male and female (ἄρσεν καὶ θῆλυ) he created them."

The second chapter of the *Book of Genesis* speaks firstly about the creation of one Man, and afterwards about the creation of Woman from his bones and his flesh: "She shall be called Woman, because she was taken out of Man" (אִשָּׁה כִּי מֵאִישׁ; Gen 2:23). The reason for this was that it was not good that man should be alone (LXX, Gen 2:18: μόνος). Therefore, a man leaves his father and his mother, and cleaves to his wife, and they become one flesh (LXX, Gen 2:24: σάρξ μία).

These two texts seem to speak about one Man (ἄνθρωπος), perhaps considered as a human being in general, and created in the image (εἰκών) of God. However this image is expressed more precisely in the unity between Man and Woman (ἄρσην καὶ θῆλυς). In some way they become merged into one body (σάρξ μία).

In addition to this, the biblical text relates that when the man and the woman were in the Garden of Eden they were both naked and not ashamed (Gen 2:25), and that they could freely eat of every tree in the garden including from the tree of life, but not from the tree of knowledge of good and evil, which would cause their death (Gen 2:16-17; 3:3).

We can find some echoes of these texts in the New Testament. The *Gospel of Matthew* (22:23-33) presents a discussion between the Sadducees and Jesus regarding resurrection. Seven brothers, one after another, married the same woman and then died. According to the Sadducees there will be a problem after their resurrection; namely, whose wife will she be? Jesus answers them by challenging their knowledge of both the scriptures and the power of God. For "in the resurrection they neither marry nor are given in marriage, but are like angels in heaven (ὡς ἄγγελοι ἐν τῷ οὐρανῷ εἰσιν; Mat 22:30)."

This text reveals that the power of God is able to transform the human person into something like that of an angel, possibly indicating a new gender which is neither male nor female but something encompassing both. However, to describe this new reality in the Kingdom of heaven, the Gospel uses images borrowed from human life reflecting the polarity of man and woman (ex. Mat 25:1-13). Saint Paul will also touch on this issue in his letter to the Ephesians: "For no man ever hates his own flesh, but nourishes and cherishes it, as Christ does the church, because we are members of his body. *For this reason a man shall leave his father and mother and be joined to his wife, and the two shall become one flesh.* This mystery is a profound one, and I am saying that it refers to Christ and the church" (Eph 5:29-33). According to this text, the mystery of Christ and his Church is an accomplishment of the mystery of one body created by Man and Woman described in the *Book of Genesis*.

On the basis of this idea Paul elaborated his doctrine of the one body of Christ composed of many members (cf. 1 Co 12:12-30; Rom 12:4-5; Gal 3:26-27). Now "there is neither Jew nor Greek, there is neither slave nor free, there is neither male nor female (ἄρσεν καὶ θῆλυ); for you are all one (εἷς) in Christ Jesus" (Gal 3:28). However, although the pure bride has been betrothed to Christ her only husband, Paul is afraid that as the serpent deceived Eve by his cunning, her thoughts will be led astray from a sincere and pure devotion to her husband, Christ (2 Cor 11:2-3). This is another reference to Man and Woman in the *Book of Genesis*. In this context a question immediately arises: how is it possible to show in human life the love between the pure bride (the Church) and her husband (Jesus)?

Paul will be the first to answer this question. In his opinion, it is better for a man not to touch a woman but to live as Paul himself did (as a celibate), in order to be free from the anxieties of this life and to be concerned only with the affairs of the Lord. In consequence, those who deal with the world should live as though they had no dealings with it. "For the form of this world is passing away". However, Paul is aware that it is impossible for everyone to live in this way, and so he only offers this as an advice to Christians, and not as an order from the Lord (1 Co 7).

An analysis of Coptic monastic texts shows that the first Christian monks wanted to recreate this state of Man and Woman in the Garden, lost after their first sin, by a certain way of life. The monks believed, it seems, that it was possible to return to the very beginning of human existence in order to find the unity between male and female in one body.

Solitary life of monks

In the history of Christianity we can find at least two ways in which these ideals were practiced. The first was life in community, which seems to be nearest to Paul's idea. The second involved those who wanted to realize their love for Christ as monks in the desert, living more or less solitary lives. The common link between these two ways of monastic living was the conviction that it was impossible to love both the world and God together. To realize this ideal it was necessary to leave the "world" and to begin a new life in order to create something new, a new person. The preferred place to accomplish this task was the desert.

Demetrius of Antioch

In the Coptic tradition, the life of desert monks was often presented to people as the ideal Christian life. For example we find this in a Coptic homily, *On the Nativity*[1] attributed to Demetrius, a bishop of Antioch[2]. The version we now have was probably composed in the seventh century, but it is based on more ancient texts. At the end of the homily the author invites his audience to conversion. By this he means the common monastic ideal, namely that it was necessary to abandon completely one's former way of life and to undergo a kind of transformation. To express this Demetrius quotes a biblical passage from the *Book of Proverbs*: "Prepare your work outside, get everything ready for you in the field; and after that build your house."[3] The text of the homily is as follow: "Hearken unto Salomon, the Wise, as he cries out to you: Make ready your things for your road and you will build a house for you for ever. Abandon the first things, hold the armor of salvation and follow Jesus Christ, in order to make a new building."[4]

Afterwards, Demetrius advises his audience to go outside the city to a monastery in order to see the monks, who were once sinners themselves, but who have now abandoned their evil way of life and have be-

---

[1] Ed. K. Modras, *Omelia copta attribuita a Demetrio di Antiochia sul Natale et Maria Vergine*, in *Unione Accademica Nazionale, Corpus dei Manoscritti Copti Letterari*, Roma 1994. We have the homily in three manuscripts, two from the Morgan Library (M596 and M597) and one from the British Library (BL7027).

[2] It seems that Flavian, bishop of Antioch, was known as Demetrius by the Coptic Church in the second half of the fourth century. It was he who ordained John Chrysostom as priest. Cf. K. Modras, *Omelia copta...*, p. 25-26.

[3] Pro 24:27: C̄BTE NEK2BHYE ETEK2IH· ⲀYⲰ N̄C̄BTⲰTK ETEKCⲰⲰE N̄ⲄOYⲀ2K N̄CⲰI· ⲀYⲰ KNⲀKⲰT M̄ⲠEKHÏ: Cf. G.P.G. Sobhy, *The Book of the Proverbs of Solomon* (Cairo 1927, p. ⲧⲓⲋ). M597 and BL7027 are more faithful than M596 to the biblical text. Cf. also the text of BHS and LXX:

BHS: הָכֵן בַּחוּץ מְלַאכְתֶּךָ וְעַתְּדָהּ בַּשָּׂדֶה לָךְ אַחַר וּבָנִיתָ בֵיתֶךָ׃

LXX: ἑτοίμαζε εἰς τὴν ἔξοδον τὰ ἔργα σου καὶ παρασκευάζου εἰς τὸν ἀγρὸν καὶ πορεύου κατόπισθέν μου καὶ ἀνοικοδομήσεις τὸν οἶκόν σου.

The texts are slightly different, however all of them contain the idea of going out, which was the beginning of a new life.

[4] M596, 883-884: CⲰTM ECOⲖOMⲰN ⲠCⲰ̄ⲪOC· EⲩⲰⲰ EBOⲖ EPⲰTN· ⲬE CEBTE NEK2BHYE ETEK2IH· ⲀYⲰ KNⲀKⲰT NOYHÏ NⲀK ⲰⲀ ENE2: TϬⲒNⲀⲠOTⲀCCE ⲄⲀP N̄NEK2BHYE N̄ⲰOPⲠ· TⲠⲀN2ⲰⲠⲖⲒⲀ M̄ⲠOYⲬⲀÏ· N̄ⲄOYⲀ2K̄ NCⲀ ⲠNⲬOEIC ⲒC̄ ⲠEⲬC̄· ⲬEKⲀC EKEEP OYKⲰT N̄BPPE: The Coptic text is not very clear. My translation follows the version of M597, which makes more sense.

come "equal to the angels (ⲁⲩϣⲱⲡⲉ ⲛ̄ϨⲓⲤⲟⲤ ⲘⲚ ⲚⲀⲄⲄⲉⲗⲟⲤ; M596: 908-910)." After their conversion the monks received a good name and their evil deeds were covered up on the earth (M596: 907).

We recognize in this text many ideals of early Christian theology in which the love of the world and the love of God were irreconcilable. To become a new kind of person (equal to angels with a new name), the companion of Christ must abandon his way of living in this world, i.e. the city with its evil models for human life (the theatre, sexual love and fornication) in order to build something new.

Onnophrios

Among many stories of the lives of monks which the Coptic tradition has transmitted to us we have *The life of apa Onnophrios, the anchorite*[5]. This text belongs to the type called *historiae monachorum*. The author, who presents himself as Paphnutius of Scetis, during his travels in the desert between Oxyrhynchus and Shmun met some monks: Timothy, Onnophrios and four anchorites who lived in community. The historical frame of these stories corresponds to that of the second half of the fourth century[6].

Timothy was a member of a congregation of monks in Thebais, but he decided to live as an anchorite. He used to give away money that he earned by manual labor[7]. However, the Devil became envious of him and sent him a nun. After many meetings they began to eat together, and at last "brought forth death, and produced iniquity". After six months Timothy rose suddenly and went away into the desert. He owned nothing, neither clothing nor bread. There he found a spring of water, a palm-tree and a cave. The palm-tree yielded twelve bunches of dates each year, a bunch for each month. His cloths were worn out and his only covering was his own hair. He lived this way for thirty years. At

---

[5] Ed. E.A.W. Budge, *Coptic Martyrdoms*, London 1914, 205-224; 454-473.

[6] Cf. T. Orlandi, *Vite di monaci copti*, in *Collana di Testi Patristici* 41, Roma 1984, 24.

[7] Budge, *The life of apa Onnophrius...* fol. 3a: "A thought of this kind came into my heart: Rise up, go forth, and remain in your place by yourself. And you shall be at rest and become an anchorite (ⲁⲩⲱ ⲔⲚⲀⲉⲤⲨⲬⲀⲌⲉ ⲙ̄ⲘⲟⲔ Ⲛⲅ̄ⲀⲚⲀⲬⲱⲣⲉⲓ), and shall receive the brethren to you. You shall become very hospitable, and you shall find an abundant wage by the work of your hands."

first he suffered greatly, but after a miracle of healing he lived without any pain. The blessing Timothy gave Paphnutius was so efficacious that he no longer felt hunger or thirst (fol. 2a-6a).

The second monk whom Paphnutius met was Onnophrios (fol. 6a-15b) who lived in a perfect monastic community in Shmun[8]. However, after reading about the life of the prophet Elijah and John the Baptist, he decided to leave the easy life of the monastery for a solitary life in the desert. The text indicates that he looked for a special power given by God to those who undertook ascetic labors. The text quotes the prophet Isaiah: "Those who abide in the Lord shall renew their strength, they shall become winged like the eagles, they shall run and shall not fall, they shall walk and shall not suffer hunger (fol. 8a; Is 40,31)." This story also recounts that a palm-tree which after yielding one bunch of dates every month as nourishment for Onnophrios (fol. 11a) fell over after his death (fol. 15b), thus indicating that the state of the monk was something personal and not transferable to others. During his life in the desert Onnophrios was also naked, covered only with leaves (fol. 6a), in response to the word of Jesus who said that one should not be anxious about what one shall eat, drink or wear, for the heavenly Father knows all that one needs. Let him rather seek first his kingdom and its right-eousness, and all these things shall be his as well (fol. 11a-11b; cf. Mt 6,31-33).

The last story tells about four monks: John, Andrew, Heraklamon and Theophilus, who lived near a well of water which had large fruit-trees of all kinds (fol. 17a-20b). This time unlike Timothy and Onno-phrios, these monks were described as being handsome, clean and well dressed (fol. 17b: ENECⲰOY 2Ⲛ TEYⲌIKⲰN) in fine skin garments, which covered their entire bodies. "They remained in a state of great rest, like those who had transferred themselves to another world, in their joy and their consolation, shown towards me" (Fol. 17b). They were sons of the magistrates of the city of Oxyrhynchus, well educated in the wisdom of the world. However, they wished to be instructed also in the

---

[8] Fol. 7a: "We were together of the same heart (ENO ⲚOY2HT ⲚOYⲰT MⲚ NEN-EPHY 2I OYCOⲠ), and the peace dwelt in our midst. We were together at rest (2Ⲛ OYECYXIⲀ), glorifying God. I used to pass nights in vigil with them, learning the rules of God from them; they were perfect, as the angels of the Lord (ⲚOE ⲚⲚAⲅⲅE-ⲖOC ⲘⲠⲬC)."

wisdom of God, and by the decision of their inner man they left the city and lived as a group of solitaries in the desert[9].

In all three stories we find some interesting ideas about hermitical life, which is presented as superior to life in community. Those who desire to become monks must leave the world behind completely and go into the desert. At first the anchorite will experience profound struggles with the Devil in many different ways. In the story of Timothy, this struggle appears as sexual temptation for a woman. In other cases, the texts speak about hunger, thirst, hostile weather or illness. After a time, the monk experiences freedom from all contingencies, and as a solitary, he lives naked, without pain and gifted with divine strength. His food is provided monthly by a palm-tree next to a spring of water. Timothy and Onnophrios lived alone in a garden while the other four monks lived as solitaries in community. All of them arrived at a complete transformation of their personality and body, no longer experiencing suffering or passions. This new state was often referred to in the monastic tradition as ἡσυχία. The monk moves into a new world symbolized by the tree of life in the biblical Garden of Eden (cf. Ap 22:1-2; Ez 47:12).

Paul of Tamma

In the second half of the fourth century we read about a monk called Paul of Tamma[10], a solitary living in the region between Memphis and Shmun. He is important for Coptic monastic tradition because of the written works he himself left us[11], unlike other biographies written by visitors and not by the monks themselves.

Paul of Tamma proposes a solitary kind of life in the silence of the monastic cell. He gives the following advice in his *Epistula*: "Don't give rest to your thoughts, until the rest will become for you unrestful. Leave

---

[9] Fol. 18a-b: "A good thought operated in our inner man. We rose all four, and we went to the mountain to be at rest (ⲉⲧⲣⲛ̄ⲉⲥⲩⲭⲁⲍⲉ ⲙ̄ⲙⲟⲛ), until we should see what the Lord would ordain for us."

[10] Ed. T. Orlandi, *Paolo di Tamma, Opere. Introduzione, testo, traduzione e concordanze*, Roma 1988.

[11] In the edition of T. Orlandi, we find *Epistula, De cella, De iudicio, De paupertate* and *De humilitate* and *Sine titolo*.

the thoughts die and live in the affairs of God."[12] The monk needs to rest from thoughts and to be free of all bonds (*Opus sine titulo*, 115), without any worries or much activity (*De paupertate*, 2-4). Only the solitary monk in his cell in the desert can arrive at this new, happy and powerful state of existence (*De cella*, 119-122). It comes from the presence of God with the monk in his cell. His body becomes a temple of God[13]. His soul and his thoughts constantly contemplate God in the monastic cell (*De Cella*, 77) where he sees the image of God within himself[14]. This state of life is described as the season of love, in which "the voice of the turtledove called in your land among us (cf. Sol 2:12), inside your place of rest"[15]. It is a New Jerusalem with an abundance of goods and a well of water (*De Humilitate*, 24). All these ideas send us back to the Book of Genesis (Gen 1:26-27; 5:1; 9:6) and indicate the goal of monastic living in the desert[16].

---

[12] *Epistula*, 3: ΝΕΚΜΕΕΥΕ ΔΕ ΜΠΡΤ ΜΤΟΝ ΝΑΥ ϢΑΝΤΕ ΠΕΜΤΟΝ ϢⲰΠΕ ΝΑΚ ΕΧΜ ΠΕΜΤΟ(Ν)· ΕΚΕΚΑΑΥ ΕΥΜΟΟΥΤ ΕΚΟΝ2 2Ν ΝΑ ΠΝΟΥΤΕ:

[13] Cf. *Opus sine titulo*, 112: ΑΛΛΑ ΕΡ ΠΕΚⲤⲰΜΑ ΝΕΡΠΕ ΜΠΝΟΥΤΕ ΝΓΕΡΧ ΝΕΚΜΕΕΥⲈ ΤΑΡΕΚΧΠΟ ΝΑΚ ΜΠΜΕΕΥΕ ΕΤⲤΜΟΝΤ: "Make your body a temple of God, bind your thoughts and you will acquire for you the firm thought."

[14] *De Cella*, 24: ΚΑ ΝΕΚΒΑΛ ΕΠΕⲤΗΤ ΝⲐΙΚⲰΝ ΜΠΝΟΥΤΕ ΝⲐΕ ΝΝΙΕⲤΟΟΥ: Cf. also, *De Cella, 64*, ver. MU0166 (Orlandi, p. 96): ΚΑ ΠΕΚΜΕΕΥΕ 2ΙΠΕⲤΗΤ ΕΚΠΙⲤΤΕΥΕ ΧΕ ΟΥΝ ⲤΚΟΠΟⲤ ϢΟΟΠ ΝⲐΙΚⲰΝ ΜΠΝΟΥΤΕ: or ver. MONB.GU (Orlandi, 104): ΚΑ ΠΕΚΜΕΥΕ ΕΠΕⲤΗΤ ΝΡⲰΜΕ ΝΙΜ ΕΚΠΙⲤΤΕΥΕ ΧΕ ΟΥΝ ⲤΚΟΠΟⲤ ϢΟΟΠ ΝⲐΙΚⲰΝ ΜΠΝΟΥΤΕ: It is probably a matter of the anthropomorphic controversy about the image of God in man. Cf. T. Orlandi, *Paolo di Tamma*... p. 15.

[15] *Epistula*, 6: ΑΠΕ2ΡΟΟΥ ΜΠΕⲞΡΜϢΑΝ ΜΟΥΤΕ 2Μ ΠΕΚΚΑ2· 2Ι2ΟΥΝ ΜΜΟΝ Ε2ΟΥΝ ΕΠΕΚΜΑΝΜΤΟΝ 2ΑΜΗΝ:

[16] Cf. T. Orlandi, *Vita di Aphu*, in *Vite di monaci copti*, in A. Quacquarelli, *Collana di testi patristici*, 41, Roma 1984, 51-65. This is a story of a monk, Aphou of Pemgje (Oxyrhynchus), from the second half of the fourth century. He went to Alexandria to correct an expression of the patriarch Theophilus in his Easter letter. Theophilus would not have recognized the image of God in all men (only in Adam) in order to elevate the glory of God and to recall the inferiority of men. According to Aphou, this sentence did not agree with the Book of Genesis. The weak nature of man can be an image of the great glory of God, as a picture is a true image of a king. We do not know if the dispute of Aphou with Theophilus is true; in any case, such an origenistic controversy at the time of Theophilus is a historical fact (years 399-400). The negation of the image of God in men could have shaken the motivation of the monastic asceticism. Cf. T. Orlandi, *Vita di Aphu*..., p.51-53.

Gospel of Thomas

While reflecting on the nature of the image of God hidden in every human person we cannot overlook the *Gospel of Thomas*[17], which was among the texts discovered at Nag Hammadi in 1945. We have fragments of this text which were composed in Greek, probably during the first decade of the second century (100-110 CE), but its oldest core may have originated many decades earlier (60-70 CE). The final Coptic version we now have was produced in the fourth century CE[18].

The *Gospel of Thomas* offers 114 sayings of Jesus for personal meditation or for community reflection. Some of these sayings have parallels in the canonical Gospels. Some of them are known from other sources, while others are completely new.

In the *Gospel of Thomas,* I have identified many ideas which eventually provided a theological basis for monastic asceticism. The person who wants to become a monk (i.e. solitary) must leave this world behind completely (Sayings 21, 27, 42, 47, 60, 71, 98). The term "world" contains all the traditional categories, like social (37, 64, 78), familial (16, 55, 79, 99, 101, 105) religious (6, 14, 27, 52, 53) and material wealth (63, 76, 81, 110). Those who live in the midst of these things are drunk and blind. They do not see that they have come into the world (κόσμος) empty and that they will leave it empty. Therefore a conversion (μετανοεῖν) is necessary (28). The new existence consists in becoming a small child again (4, 22, 46), and in recreating a new society built on the basis of new categories (15, 22, 27, 37, 50, 53, 99, 101, 111). The old world is not worthy of this new person (56, 80, 111) who has past into a new state of existence in which he no longer tastes death (1, 11, 18, 19, 111) because he has finally entered the place of real life (4). This place is at the beginning (ἀρχή)[19], in Paradise in which there is no change[20];

---

[17] Ed. A. Guillaumont, H.-Ch. Puech, G. Quispel, W. Till and Yassah Abd Al Masih, *The Gospel according to Thomas. Coptic text established and translated,* Leiden and New York 1959.

[18] Cf. R. Valantasis, *The Gospel of Thomas,* London and New York 1997, 12-21, 49-50.

[19] Saying 18: "The disciples said to Jesus: Tell us how our end will be. Jesus said: Have you then discovered the beginning (ⲁⲣⲭⲏ) so that you inquire about the end? For where the beginning (ⲁⲣⲭⲏ) is, there shall be the end. Blessed is he who shall stand at

where clothes are no longer necessary, and in which the new person is no longer ashamed[21]. This is a place of rest (ἀνάπαυσις; 50). This new world is already present (51, 113), because the kingdom (light, spirit and great wealth) is within the one who has knowledge (3, 5, 24, 29, 51, 70). He knows himself (3, 67, 111) and their image and their origin are manifest to him.

> **Saying 50**: Jesus said: If they say to you: «From where have you originated?», say to them: «We have come from the Light, where the Light has originated through itself. It (stood) and it revealed itself in their image». If they say to you: «(Who) are you?», say: «We are His sons and we are the elect of the Living Father». If they ask you: «What is the sign of your Father in you?», say to them: «It is a movement and a rest»"[22].
>
> **Saying 83**: Jesus said: The images are manifest to man and the Light, which is within them, is hidden in the Image of the Light of the Father. He will manifest himself and His image is hidden by His Light[23].
>
> **Saying 84**: Jesus said: When you see your likeness, you rejoice. But when you see your images which came into existence before you, (which) neither die nor are manifested, how much will you bear![24].

Adam came into existence from a great power and from great wealth, but the monk after the process of transformation supercedes Adam in dignity because he has tasted death (85).

---

the beginning (ⲁⲣⲭⲏ), and he shall know the end and he shall not taste death." Cf. Sayings 19, 49.

[20] Saying 19: "For you have five trees in Paradise, which are unmoved in summer (or) in winter and their leaves do not fall."

[21] Saying 37: "His disciples said: When will You be revealed to us and when will we see You? Jesus said: When you take off your clothing without being ashamed, and take your clothes and put them under your feet as the little children and tread on them, then shall you behold the Son of the Living (One) and you shall not fear." Cf. Saying 36. On the contrary, those who are clothed in soft garments will not be able to know the truth (Saying 78).

[22] Saying 50: ⲡⲉϫⲉ ⲓ̅ⲥ̅ ϫⲉ ⲉⲩϣⲁⲛϫⲟⲟⲥ ⲛⲏⲧⲛ̅ ϫⲉ ⲛ̅ⲧⲁⲧⲉⲧⲛ̅ϣⲱⲡⲉ ⲉ-ⲃⲟⲗ ⲧⲱⲛ ϫⲟⲟⲥ ⲛⲁⲩ ϫⲉ ⲛ̅ⲧⲁⲛⲉⲓ ⲉⲃⲟⲗ ϩⲙ̅ ⲡⲟⲩⲟⲉⲓⲛ ⲡⲙⲁ ⲉⲛⲧⲁⲡⲟⲩⲟⲉⲓⲛ ϣⲱⲡⲉ ⲙ̅ⲙⲁⲩ ⲉⲃⲟⲗ ϩⲓⲧⲟⲟⲧϥ ⲟⲩⲁⲁⲧϥ ⲁϥⲱϩ[ⲉ ⲉⲣⲁⲧϥ] ⲁⲩⲱ ⲁϥⲟⲩⲱⲛϩ [ⲉⲃ]ⲟⲗ ϩⲛ ⲧⲟⲩϩⲓⲕⲱⲛ ⲉⲩϣⲁϫⲟⲟⲥ ⲛⲏⲧⲛ̅ ϫⲉ ⲛ̅ⲧⲱⲧⲛ̅ ⲡⲉ ϫⲟⲟⲥ ϫⲉ ⲁⲛⲟⲛ ⲛⲉϥϣⲏⲣⲉ ⲁⲩⲱ ⲁⲛⲟⲛ ⲛ̅ⲥⲱⲧⲡ ⲙ̅ⲡⲉⲓⲱⲧ ⲉⲧⲟⲛϩ ⲉⲩϣⲁⲛϫⲛⲉ ⲧⲏⲩⲧⲛ̅ ϫⲉ ⲟⲩ ⲡⲉ ⲡⲙⲁⲉⲓⲛ ⲙ̅ⲡⲉⲧⲛ̅ⲉⲓⲱⲧ ⲉⲧϩⲛ̅ ⲧⲏⲩⲧⲛ̅ ϫⲟⲟⲥ ⲉⲣⲟⲟⲩ ϫⲉ ⲟⲩⲕⲓⲙ ⲡⲉ ⲙⲛ̅ ⲟⲩⲁⲛⲁⲡⲁⲩⲥⲓⲥ·

[23] Saying 83: ⲡⲉϫⲉ ⲓ̅ⲥ̅ ϫⲉ ⲛϩⲓⲕⲱⲛ ⲥⲉⲟⲩⲟⲛϩ ⲉⲃⲟⲗ ⲙ̅ⲡⲣⲱⲙⲉ ⲁⲩⲱ ⲡ-ⲟⲩⲟⲉⲓⲛ ⲉⲧⲛ̅ϩⲏⲧⲟⲩ ϥϩⲏⲡ ϩⲛ̅ ⲑⲓⲕⲱⲛ ⲙ̅ⲡⲟⲩⲟⲉⲓⲛ ⲙ̅ⲡⲉⲓⲱⲧ ϥⲛⲁϭⲱⲗⲡ ⲉⲃⲟⲗ ⲁⲩⲱ ⲧⲉϥϩⲓⲕⲱⲛ ϩⲏⲡ ⲉⲃⲟⲗ ϩⲓⲧⲛ̅ ⲡⲉϥⲟⲩⲟⲉⲓⲛ·

[24] Saying 84: ⲡⲉϫⲉ ⲓ̅ⲥ̅ ⲛ̅ϩⲟⲟⲩ ⲉⲧⲉⲧⲛ̅ⲛⲁⲩ ⲉⲡⲉⲧⲛ̅ⲉⲓⲛⲉ ϣⲁⲣⲉⲧⲛ̅ⲣⲁϣⲉ ϩⲟⲧⲁⲛ ⲇⲉ ⲉⲧⲉⲧⲛ̅ϣⲁⲛⲛⲁⲩ ⲁⲛⲉⲧⲛ̅ϩⲓⲕⲱⲛ ⲛ̅ⲧⲁϩϣⲱⲡⲉ ϩⲓ ⲧⲉⲧⲛⲉϩⲏ ⲟⲩⲧⲉ ⲙⲁⲩⲙⲟⲩ ⲟⲩⲧⲉ ⲙⲁⲩⲟⲩⲱⲛϩ ⲉⲃⲟⲗ ⲧⲉⲧⲛⲁϥⲓ ϩⲁ ⲟⲩⲏⲣ·

This new person is called a monk or a solitary (MONAXOC), indicating someone who is single[25], not divided, because he has been engendered from the Same One and from the Light[26]. They became one God[27]. He left behind the universal division and hostility of the present world (16) and alone enters the bridal chamber[28] which is the kingdom[29].

However, the sense of "becoming the single one" is even more profound. The man became two (male and female)[30] and now a union between the two is necessary[31]. From their union, but not in marriage, a third gender arises which is neither man nor woman. This new reality is something completely recreated in all its parts according to a new image[32]:

> **Saying 22**: Jesus saw children who were being suckled. He said to his disciples: These children who are being suckled are like those who enter the Kingdom. They said to Him: Shall we then, being children, enter the Kingdom? Jesus said to them: When you make the two one, and when

---

[25] Saying 4: "Jesus said: The man old in days will not hesitate to ask a little child of seven days about the place of Life, and he will live. For many who are first shall become last and they shall become a single one (ⲚⲤⲈⲰⲰⲠⲈ ⲞⲨⲀ ⲞⲨⲰⲦ)." Saying 23: "Jesus said: I shall choose you, one out of a thousand, and two out of ten thousand, and they shall stand as a single one (ⲀⲨⲰ ⲤⲈⲚⲀⲰⲞⲢ ⲈⲢⲀⲦⲞⲨ ⲈⲨⲞ ⲞⲨⲀ ⲞⲨⲰⲦ)."

[26] Saying 61: "Jesus said: Two will rest on a bed: the one will die, the one will live. Salome said: Who are you, man, and whose (son)? You did take your place upon my bench and eat from my table. Jesus said to her: I am he who is from the Same (ⲠⲈⲦⲰⲞⲞⲠ ⲈⲂⲞⲖ ⲌⲘ ⲠⲈⲦⲰⲎⲰ), to Me was given from the things of My Father. <Salome said>: I am your disciple. <Jesus said to her>: Therefore I say, if he is the Same (ⲌⲞⲦⲀⲚ ⲈⲨⲰⲀⲰⲰⲠⲈ ⲈⲨⲰⲎ4), he will be filled with light, but if he is divided (ⲌⲞⲦⲀⲚ ⲆⲈ ⲈⲨⲰⲀⲚⲰⲰⲠⲈ ⲈⲨⲠⲎⲰ), he will be filled with darkness."

[27] Saying 30: ⲠⲈⲬⲈ ⲒⲤ ⲬⲈ ⲠⲘⲀ ⲈⲨⲚ ⲰⲞⲘⲦ ⲚⲚⲞⲨⲦⲈ ⲘⲘⲀⲨ ⲌⲚⲚⲞⲨⲦⲈ ⲚⲈ ⲠⲘⲀ ⲈⲨⲚ ⲤⲚⲀⲨ Ⲏ ⲞⲨⲀ ⲀⲚⲞⲔ ϮⲰⲞⲞⲠ ⲚⲘⲘⲀ4: "Jesus said: Where there are three gods, they are gods; where there are two or one, I am with him."

[28] Saying 75: "Jesus said: Many are standing at the door, but the solitaries (MONAXOC) are the ones who will enter the bridal chamber."

[29] Saying 49: "Jesus said: Blessed are the solitaries (MONAXOC) and elect, for you shall find he Kingdom; because you come from it, (and) you shall go there again."

[30] Saying 11: "Jesus said: This heaven shall pass away and the one above it shall pass away, and the dead are not alive and the living shall not die. In the days when you devoured the dead, you made it alive; when you come into light, what will you do? On the day when you were one, you became two (ⲌⲘ ⲪⲞⲞⲨ ⲈⲦⲈⲦⲚⲞ ⲚⲞⲨⲀ ⲀⲦⲈⲦⲚⲈⲒⲢⲈ ⲘⲠⲤⲚⲀⲨ). But when you have become two, what will you do?"

[31] Saying 106: "Jesus said: When you make the two one (ⲌⲞⲦⲀⲚ ⲈⲦⲈⲦⲚⲰⲀⲢ ⲠⲤⲚⲀⲨ ⲞⲨⲀ), you shall become sons of Man, and when you say: «Mountain, be moved», it will be moved."

[32] Cf. R. Valantasis, *The Gospel of Thomas* ..., p.95-96.

you make the inner as the outer and the outer as the inner and the above as the below, and when you make the male and the female into a single one, so that the male will not be male and the female (not) be female, when you make eyes in the place of an eye, and a hand in the place of a hand, and a foot in the place of a foot, (and) an image in the place of an image, then shall you enter (the Kingdom)[33].

Saying 114: Simon Peter said to them: Let Mary go out from among us, because women are not worthy of the Life. Jesus said: See, I shall lead her, so that I will make her male, that she too may become a living spirit, resembling you males. For every woman who makes herself male will enter the Kingdom of Heaven[34].

Conclusion

We have now returned to Paradise, to the one Human being, to a new gender in which the image of God has been recreated through asceticism and knowledge. This is the one body referred to in the *Book of Genesis*, reinterpreted by Saint Paul and the monastic tradition. There is no distinction between man and woman in this one body. The Coptic monks (the solitaries) wanted to arrive at this new state of existence through an ascetical way of living in the desert. They proposed a new understanding for the idea in the *Book of Genesis* that it is not good for man to be alone: that of a μόνος who is an image of a perfect human being, man and woman, who stands alone before God in order to contemplate God's image in himself.

Krzysztof Modras, OP

---

[33] Saying 22: ⲁⲓⲥ ⲚⲀⲨ ⲀⲊ Ⲛ̄ⲔⲞⲨⲈⲒ ⲈⲨⳢⲒ ⲈⲢⲰⲦⲈ ⲠⲈⳢⲀϤ ⲚⲚⲈϤⲘⲀⲐⲎⲦⲎⲤ ⳢⲈ ⲚⲈⲈⲒⲔⲞⲨⲈⲒ ⲈⲦⳢⲒ ⲈⲢⲰⲦⲈ ⲈⲨⲦⲚ̄ⲦⲰⲚ ⲀⲚⲈⲦⲂⲎⲔ ⲈⳢⲞⲨⲚ ⲀⲦⲘⲚ̄ⲦⲈⲢⲞ ⲠⲈⲬⲀⲨ ⲚⲀϤ ⳢⲈ ⲈⲈⲒ ⲈⲚⲞ Ⲛ̄ⲔⲞⲨⲈⲒ ⲦⲚⲚⲀⲂⲰⲔ ⲈⳢⲞⲨⲚ ⲈⲦⲘⲚ̄ⲦⲈⲢⲞ ⲠⲈⳢⲈ ⲒⲎⲤ ⲚⲀⲨ ⳢⲈ ⳢⲞⲦⲀⲚ ⲈⲦⲈⲦⲚ̄⳨ⲀⲢ̄ ⲠⲤⲚⲀⲨ ⲞⲨⲀ ⲀⲨⲰ ⲈⲦⲈⲦⲚ̄⳨ⲀⲢ̄ ⲠⲤⲀ Ⲛ̄ⳢⲞⲨⲚ Ⲛ̄ⲐⲈ Ⲙ̄ⲠⲤⲀ ⲚⲂⲞⲖ ⲀⲨⲰ ⲠⲤⲀ ⲚⲂⲞⲖ Ⲛ̄ⲐⲈ Ⲙ̄ⲠⲤⲀ Ⲛ̄ⳢⲞⲨⲚ ⲀⲨⲰ ⲠⲤⲀ (Ⲛ)ⲦⲠⲈ Ⲛ̄ⲐⲈ Ⲙ̄ⲠⲤⲀ Ⲙ̄ⲠⲒⲦⲚ̄ ⲀⲨⲰ ⳨ⲒⲚⲀ ⲈⲦⲈⲦⲚⲀⲈⲒⲢⲈ Ⲙ̄ⲪⲞⲞⲨⲦ ⲘⲚ̄ ⲦⳢⲒⲘⲈ Ⲙ̄ⲠⲒⲞⲨⲀ ⲞⲨⲰⲦ ⳢⲈⲔⲀⲀⲤ ⲚⲈϤⲞⲞⲨⲦ Ⲣ̄ ⳢⲞⲞⲨⲦ· Ⲛ̄ⲦⲈ ⲦⳢⲒⲘⲈ Ⲣ̄ ⳢⳢⲒⲘⲈ ⳢⲞⲦⲀⲚ ⲈⲦⲈⲦⲚ̄⳨ⲀⲈⲒⲢⲈ Ⲛ̄Ⲛ̄ⲂⲀⲖ ⲈⲠⲘⲀ Ⲛ̄ⲞⲨⲂⲀⲖ· ⲀⲨⲰ ⲞⲨⳒⲒⳢ ⲈⲠⲘⲀ Ⲛ̄ⲞⲨⳒⲒⳢ· ⲀⲨⲰ ⲞⲨⲈⲢⲎⲦⲈ ⲈⲠⲘⲀ Ⲛ̄ⲞⲨⲈⲢⲎⲦⲈ ⲞⲨⳢⲒⲔⲰⲚ ⲈⲠⲘⲀ Ⲛ̄ⲞⲨⳢⲒⲔⲰ(Ⲛ) ⲦⲞⲦⲈ ⲦⲈⲦⲚⲀⲂⲰⲔ ⲈⳢⲞⲨⲚ (ⲈⲦⲘⲚⲦⲈⲢⲞ).

[34] Saying 114: ⲠⲈⳢⲈ ⲤⲒⲘⲰⲚ ⲠⲈⲦⲢⲞⲤ ⲚⲀⲨ ⳢⲈ ⲘⲀⲢⲈ ⲘⲀⲢⲒⳢⲀⲘ ⲈⲒ ⲈⲂⲞⲖ Ⲛ̄ⳢⲎⲦⲚ̄ ⳢⲈ Ⲛ̄ⳢⳢⲒⲞⲘⲈ Ⲙ̄Ⲡ⳨Ⲁ ⲀⲚ Ⲙ̄ⲠⲰⲚⳢ ⲠⲈⳢⲈ ⲒⲤ ⳢⲈ ⲈⲒⲤ ⳢⲎⲎⲦⲈ ⲀⲚⲞⲔ ϮⲚⲀⲤⲰⲔ Ⲙ̄ⲘⲞⲤ ⳢⲈⲔⲀⲀⲤ ⲈⲈⲒⲚⲀⲀⲤ Ⲛ̄ⳢⲞⲞⲨⲦ· ⳨ⲒⲚⲀ ⲈⲤⲚⲀ⳨ⲰⲠⲈ ⳢⲰⲰⲤ Ⲛ̄ⲞⲨⲠⲚ̄Ⲁ ⲈϤⲞⲚⳢ ⲈϤⲈⲒⲚⲈ Ⲙ̄ⲘⲰⲦⲚ̄ Ⲛ̄ⳢⲞⲞⲨⲦ ⳢⲈ ⳢⳢⲒⲘⲈ ⲚⲒⲘ ⲈⲤⲚⲀⲀⲤ Ⲛ̄ⳢⲞⲞⲨⲦ ⲤⲚⲀⲂⲰⲔ ⲈⳢⲞⲨⲚ̄ ⲈⲦⲘⲚ̄ⲦⲈⲢⲞ ⲚⲘ̄ⲠⲎⲨⲈ·

TABLE OF CONTENTS

F-87350 PANAZOL
N° Imprimeur : 0096572-00
Dépôt légal : Décembre 2000